Not a hero in sight and a message around every corner, snippets, episodes, fragments, bits and pieces of a whole it's up to you to put them together to create the story you want to hear.

This is a novelty book of short stories. It's an odd combination of cutesy down home silliness and outright horror and cruelty which somehow comes together as utterly believable though I'm not sure if any of it is or if it is all just complete BS.

These stories (it's a very short book) are really charming, a little boy who never left his past and who will carry it to his grave.

Who cares? One more whiney-assed, over the hill creative type who thinks the world owes him something. It's a character not a person wake up get on with your life.

If you can get over the fact that the author seems to be a reprehensible misogynist, it's interesting.

Seething sarcasm written like an advertisement for a wasted life. A low rent death of a salesman.

Conley J Boyce is an asshole

Thank you patsycoo
for getting me started for the last time.

And many thanks to
the Church of Jesus Starbucks in Concord,
and to the big white couch at Koco Java in Salisbury
upon which much of this was written

Read the book this morning over tea on the porch . . .
Impressively, authentically funny
I choked myself laughing . . .
The stories were original (truth usually is) . . .
The fact that you laid yourself on the altar of judgment
is to be respected.

M.E.B. Smith

I found no proof-reading errors. Not a one.
I did find humor, but alas it was of a vulgar temperament.
Vulgar and ugly.
Some were depressing, but that was what made them true.
Vulgar, ugly and embarrassing.
I am glad to have read these stories.

A clown of a film-flam man is he.
I would expose the intelligence he denies, but that would not effect
a change of any kind and probably be more time consuming than I
aspire to devote to the undertaking.

The category is, of course, short stories.
For the life of me I can't conjure a genre, but would be more than a
little interested in what genre he thinks it should fall into.
I think I would enjoy a casual chat with the author,
but that would be plenty.
His collection will probably sell well with nary a negative review.

BooCoo

For my sister.

This book is a work of fiction.
Names, places, characters, and incidents are the product of the author's
imagination or are used fictitiously. Any resemblance to actual events,
locales or persons, living or dead, is coincidental.

CoonBoy Publishing
Edition 10102015
www.coonboy.com

ISBN-13: 978-0615885094
ISBN-10: 0615885098

Short
short stories
of my
too short life.

Conley J. Boyce

Appendix: How true?

Me

MY NAME IS CONLEY J. BOYCE and I live in a white trash house trailer down the road from the prison camp on Highway 73 a couple of miles outside of Mount Pleasant, North Carolina. Look it up.

[Google Earth 35°23'46.78"N 80°24'50.36"W]

For those of you who think you want to take a drive out to the country some weekend to soak up the atmosphere of small town southern life, keep this in mind: There is no mountain and there's not a damned thing pleasant about it.

A guy I know who moved here from Santa Monica to live with his childhood sweetheart because she has a job and he doesn't—she's a teacher, he's an actor, what else do you need to know?—says that living around here is like living in a bucket of shit.

He's right.

I was gone forty years. Now I'm back. Not much has changed. I'm not here because I want to be, and I don't have two nickels to rub together.

So what are you going to do?

Bide your time.

Fantasize.

Reminisce.

Try to make the best of it.

ભ

Conley J. Boyce

Me and My Cousin's Red Speckled Balls

ME AND MY COUSIN ROY LEE used to pee off the front porch together.

It seemed we always had to go pee at the same time, so we would run, barefoot and shirtless, to the far corner of the front porch, which was about three feet off the ground, high for us, pull down the elastic bands to our blue and white seersucker shorts and let her rip, better synchronized than the June Taylor Dancers.

This time was like all the others—except for the gobbler. A turkey rooster is called a gobbler.

You see, Roy Lee was uncircumcised, common if you were born at home like he was instead of a hospital where the doctors stood in line to make a fast buck cutting off the end of your pecker. Not only was Roy Lee uncircumcised, he had an unusually long foreskin. At least it looked long to me but it was the only one I'd ever seen. It hung a good inch beyond the end of the rest of it and when he peed it swirled around in circles like an out of control water hose.

It was too much for the gobbler to resist.

Even though he looked like he was too fat to fly, the turkey somehow managed to hover right in front of Roy Lee's flopping foreskin and latch on to it for brunch.

You never heard so much screaming.

Roy Lee was shaking his hands above his head and

jumping up and down, jumping and waving and screaming bloody murder.

I thought it was funny.

Roy Lee did not.

The gobbler held on, flapping his wings in time with Roy Lee's jitterbugging, buzzing right in front of him like a thirty pound overweight hummingbird.

I didn't know what to do. I remember looking at the turkey and him looking back at me with this sort of grin on his face like he was saying, you next.

I'd decided to make a run for it when the screen door slammed and out come Roy Lee's mamma whacking at the gobbler with a broom. Roy Lee screamed even louder, jitterbugged even faster. Blood curdling screams. Help me I'm dying screams. Two more whacks, this time with the broom handle, and the turkey spit it out, eyed it again, decided it's not worth it, turned and trotted away.

It started quick and it ended quick, the turkey bruised and on the run and Roy Lee squatting on the porch, his prepuce swelling up like a big, red strawberry.

There was no mending. No maternal bonding from Aunt Sis. No, Oh my sweet little baby, let mama see, does it hurt, baby baby, it's gonna be okay. None of that shit. Just turn around, go back to sweeping the floor, gone as quickly as she had come. That's life. Get used to it.

Come the afternoon and me and Roy Lee would go pick blackberries, stomping in fresh cow piles along the way, warm and squishy between our toes. We'd usually give them the one-foot stomp. But when we found one that was extra fresh and maybe a double or a triple plop, we'd give it the two-foot stomp, in unison, to see how far we could make it fly, which it did, in every direction. There was no running water at Aunt Sis's so we'd wash it off in the pond in the middle of the pasture—idyllic, halcyon days to be sure.

I never liked blackberries much, never liked to pick blackberries at all. The thorns were vicious, especially on bare, four year old skin, but the red jiggers were even worse.

Red jiggers are tiny red spiders that burrow into soft skin and then stick out a long proboscis, which is their nose, in order to breathe. They'll fester up and pop out eventually but in the meantime they itch like a son of a bitch.

On grownups they seem to prefer the arm pits, not sure why. On us it was the scrotum, soft as marshmallows.

Starting on our naked feet or legs they'd work their way up with no reason to crawl any higher and then dig in by the dozens, raising puss filled welts which caused your pouch to swell to twice its normal size.

You had two choices, either sit in a tub of cold water and Epsom Salts for hours waiting for them to drown while your pickled peter pruned up to nothing, or have your buddy stoop down real close so he could focus in on them and dab them with a spot of nail polish, which dried instantly, sealed off their airways and killed them in no time. The specks of polish would flake off a couple of days later.

We didn't have time to soak 'em out, too much to do, cow piles awaited.

Me and Roy Lee were comrades in arms, fighting the good fight with our balls as the battleground. Everywhere there was an itchy air hole on the other guy's balls, you'd hit it with a dab of Aunt Betty's bright red Maybelline fingernail polish which she kept hid in the second drawer from the top under her Saturday night underpants.

Unbeknownst to us at that young age, we were already practicing Sun Tzu's Six Principles in the Art of War. It was us against the dug in, itchy little invaders. We started with Sun's Guiding Principle Number 1: Prepare the Battlefield So That One May Achieve Perfect Victory Without Destroying It.

Pow! Pow! Pow!

Our little red bug bombs hit their targets.

Ka-pow! Ka-pow!

Our killing fields still hung proud.

Ka-pow! Hit 'em where it hurts, the sort of hand to hand combat that hasn't changed since the dawn of man.

Roy Lee never could read or write too good and dropped out of school long before he was supposed to be able to. Nobody cared. And so, just a few years later, his lack of even a basic education made him an ideal candidate to be drafted for Viet Nam, which they wasted no time in doing, and he was killed there, for no good reason whatsoever, and I never saw him again.

And I have never forgiven the government of the United States of America for that.

Not for one minute.

And I never will.

☙

Me and My Addiction

I SAT IN THE BACK, AS FAR BACK, as far away from the teacher as you could get, beside Buster Wilburn who collected bits of crayons which he kept in a crumpled up paper bag.

It was against the school law to possess bits of crayons, since each of us was issued a fresh box of eight on the first day of school and they were expected to last all year and damn the child who would break one.

Red.

Orange.

Yellow.

Blue.

Green.

Brown.

Black.

Which one am I forgetting?

No matter. There weren't enough colors. So Buster would scavenge around his big sister's bedroom and break off inch long pieces from her jumbo pack of 64 that she had gotten for her birthday.

Magenta and Pink.

Turquoise and Lime.

And the Metallics, Gold and Silver and Copper even though I didn't know what Copper was for.

Mind you, we could never use them for our daily

school project, which was illustrating the topic of a story we copied from the blackboard, stories about dogs and cats and tulips and katydids.

Getting creative with your colors was just too risky. Buster had been busted before and it took him weeks to replenish his stash, which was hidden in the far back end of the desk behind week-old corners of peanut butter and baloney sandwiches, which he used to throw off the scent.

One day, about the middle of the year, the topic was frogs, bullfrogs. It is hard to draw a bullfrog. Just ask Leonardo. Or my fellow classmates. Dogs, cats, tulips, katydids, anybody could draw one. Not the frog. Too many curvy lines. No matter how hard they worked at it, their frogs just ended up mush, a flat, green blob.

My frog was not.

On my frog, a sharp outline defined not just the overall shape but the short front legs and the muscular rear haunches—with just a suggestion of web between the toes. For the highlights and midtones, I shaded the white underbelly with a gradient, gradually mixing the White, which was in fact the white of the paper itself, into a faint undercoat of Lime. For the shadows, I rubbed in a deep layer of Crayola Standard Green before drilling in the spots on his back with Buster's last bits of Copper Metallic.

It croaked right off the page.

It was time to reflect, that time when you step back, observe what you have created and view it with an objective eye, when you ask yourself, I may have *rendered* the frog, but have I captured the essence of the frog? I had not. Something was missing. My frog had dull eyes, at least the one you could see.

(You could only see one eye. The other eye was on the other side of its head.) Most of the kids would put both eyes on the same side, a childish, innocent, Picassoesque sort of thing. I, on the other hand, was already well into my early photorealist period.

Still, my drawing lacked life and I knew that life is to be found in the eyes, even on a frog. I reached blindly into Buster's paper sack and pulled out Magenta, totally unrealistic for sure, but two violent strokes later—slash— slash—and instead of merely hopping away, the frog croaked, bounced, bounded, leapt right off the page, out the window and back into the farm pond from which it had slithered. It was masterful, and marked that seminal moment when I moved from the mundane into the infinitely wondrous—abstract expressionism.

Buster, my newfound agent, was impressed and passed my masterpiece around the room for all the other untalented eight-year olds to admire.

Frustrated by her complete lack of artistic ability, Ava, who was good at arithmetic—bright, but in the wrong sort of way—asked me to do one for her. Having already defined the creature in time and space, mentally projecting it onto an imaginary three-axis grid which sat upon the two-dimensional paper space, I whipped off a copy on the top of her page in no time.

Then Betsy.

Then Eddie.

Then Harold Blackwinder but I didn't do one for Harold Blackwinder because he was an asshole.

Marilyn.

Tommy.

Prissy-assed Cathy Blackwinder, some relation to Harold, made it known that she would do her own. Like really, do I care?

Old Lady Pruitt didn't approve.

In a big way.

She did not approve of the line of begging, pleading clients who had taken station in front of Buster's desk, awaiting their audience with The Master.

She did not approve of their cheating, not doing their own work, taking the easy way out.

And she goddamned sure did not approve of magenta eyes on a frog.

The gig was up.

The game was over.

Buster's poke full of bits and pieces was trashed once more, demonstrably this time, with a challenge to any child who should be so bold as to retrieve them from the trash basket by her desk, her sacred trash basket that none of us would ever dare violate.

But my die in life had been cast. The respect and recognition that fanciful sketch garnered me was my drug, more exhilarating than anything I had experienced in life so far.

They wanted *me*.

No, they *needed* me.

They stood in line to receive what I had to offer. Me. Me! The runt with the floppy ears, the dark circles under his eyes, the festered sore in his nose and the coon bites that never healed. They wanted me. Me, me, me, me, me.

From that day forward, I was an artist. From that day, that moment, I can trace a direct line from where I am here, now—to there, then. I've traveled from the back row to the front row and back again, with nothing to show for it in between other than a half dozen boxes of awards and the begrudging admiration of people who matter less and less as time passes, none of whom are willing now to throw a few bucks my way. I am an angry man, destroyed by Photoshop.

It's true, like it or not, that our worth to society is measured by money and money alone. And the irony is, it takes more money to escape society than it does to stay in it, no matter which row you sit on.

Crayolas were my gateway drug.

Buster traveled a different path. Buster grew up. Buster sold weed. Buster learned to keep his head low, his shit to himself and not to trust anybody who didn't sit on the back row.

His pot, not surprisingly, was mostly seeds and stems but it was enough for me and my fellow traveler and artiste, John Mourer, to attempt to get high on for the first time.

I was home from college—studying textile technology so that I could learn to exploit the common man as he toiled away in the mill—with no car and no way to go. John was home from Berklee School of Music where he was on scholarship to become the next Herb Alpert. John was a brilliant trumpet player. He made enough money during high school playing for the Saturday Night Drunks at the Shriners Club to buy a one-year old Oldsmobile

Toranado, two tons of front wheel drive and pop up headlights, the car Ferdy Porsche called the most significant American automobile of the twentieth century.

It was the Starship Enterprise and it was my ride out of town.

Navy Blue on the inside.

Copper Metallic on the outside.

Miss September in the glove box.

As I gently opened her up and spread Miss Angela Dorian (who loved animals and disliked judgmental people) across my lap, I could not help but notice that the nipples on her firm, round breasts had been airbrushed a subtle shade of Magenta.

I had an eye for that sort of thing.

Still do.

CR

Me and Spinning Dead Babies

MY AUNT SIS WAS married to a man called Screwball. Screwball wasn't his real name of course but everybody, including his own kids, called him Screwball. A couple of people, when telling Screwball stories, would refer to him, not affectionately, as The Screw.

The Screw was a scrawny wiry little weasel of a man, Barney Fife with nothing good about him.

Sis and Screwball had 12 or 13 kids. Number 3 or 4 was Marvin.

Marvin was a scrawny wiry little weasel of a man, Barney Fife with nothing good about him. He took a lot after Screwball.

At 16, Marvin married Patsy and they had four kids by the time she was a little more than 19 with another one on the way, common for the time.

They lived in a little two bedroom frame house with asbestos shingles, a little four by four foot concrete stoop in the front and a little four by four foot concrete stoop in the back.

Patsy was blond and pudgy, kind of pretty, ordinary, with nowhere to go even though she always knew she wanted to be somewhere else. She'd seen Florida on the television, Kissimmee and Koochime, water skiing and orange groves, alligators and pink flamingos. It all looked good to her.

Marvin was usually off at work with Mavin, his older brother, down at Myrtle Beach doing construction, away from home five days a week except sometimes he stayed on weekends too. Meisenheimer, where Patsy and the kids lived was not Myrtle Beach. It was not Miami Beach. It was not any beach at all.

Why not, why not for just a couple of days, she wouldn't be no trouble, she just wanted to see it, just see what it was like, see all that water, see those people laying on the sand with their bathing suits on, she didn't have to have a bathing suit, she just wanted to see it, please, please, she could leave the kids with Sis, just one time, why not, she wouldn't be no trouble, please, I just want to go, just one time, please why not?

A little two bedroom, frame house with asbestos shingles, a four by four foot concrete stoop in the front and a little four by four foot concrete stoop in the back.

Blond and pudgy.

Kind of pretty.

Four kids, aged not quite one, two, three and almost five, with another one on the way.

They cried a lot, especially the youngest, the baby. Maybe he didn't cry any more than the others but he cried, and with three more who were still of crying age, Patsy got to where she just couldn't stand the crying. She cried too.

When she bounced the baby, it would quit crying. When she spun the baby around, whee, whee, it would quit crying. Only, when she stopped and put it down, it would cry again. And then the others would cry too and she just couldn't stand the crying.

When she spun the baby around holding on to its heels, the baby would stop crying. Whe. Whee. Wheee. Spin the baby, mommy. Round and round. And the kids would laugh and jump and spin around too, whee, whee, spin the baby, whee, whee. And everybody would stop crying and laugh and squeal.

It was a little two bedroom frame house with a couch in the living room and beside the couch was an end table and on the end table was a lamp.

And the baby hit the lamp.

And the lamp fell down.

And the kids laughed and spun round and round with their arms stretched out, spinning round just like the baby, just like the baby, mommy, just like the baby.

And everybody kept spinning.

And then the baby hit something that was setting on the coffee table that sat in the middle of the room, as the baby spun round and round, now up and down and up and down.

Whee. Whee.

The baby died.

I was big enough I could see in the casket without anyone lifting me up.

They said it had died when Patsy slipped and fell on top of it as she carried it down the small, slick, back stoop. You could even see the bruises caused by the edge of the steps from underneath the makeup they had put on the baby. A deputy sheriff had conducted a thorough investigation and determined that those were the facts.

The oldest child, a girl, the one who was almost five, had talked about how they liked to see the baby spin and how the baby would quit crying and how the baby hit the lamp and made the lamp break but she was only a kid and kids made those things up. It was dead and she slipped on that slippery little bitty back stoop and she was sorry and that was what happened and nobody was going to say otherwise and if they thought something else they kept it to themselves or only talked about it in the car on the way home from the funeral, not really caring whether their kids heard it or not because we always knew Patsy was crazy and it was awful for her to do Marvin that way. He deserved better, working so hard like he did all week away from home, sometimes not even able to come home on the weekends.

Six months after that and Marvin was in a car with his brother Mavin and Patsy's mamma was in the back seat and it was late at night and they were chasing Patsy who had took Marvin's car even though she knew she wasn't supposed to.

Patsy ran the stop sign where Millingport Road crosses across Highway 73 and Marvin ran through the stop sign right behind her.

According to Patsy's mamma, Marvin had to slam on the brakes to keep from hitting a tractor trailer truck that was coming from the Mt. Pleasant side headed towards Albemarle and he spun out and hit the big oak tree over on the right, the one that stood beside the service station and was killed instantly when his head hit the front pillar of the windshield. Her and Mavin was okay. That's how Patsy's momma told it.

As people told it at Marvin's funeral, which they didn't have in the house where the baby died but at the funeral home instead, Patsy didn't stop until she got to Florida so they never could find her, but according to the deputy, she wasn't doing anything wrong anyway since the car was legally registered in her name, not Marvin's, and it didn't matter what nobody said, legally, it was her car, so there was no need to look for her and nobody ever knew for sure what happened to her or where she was, but they didn't really care anyhow just as long as she was gone and never came back and they never heard from her again.

By the time the accident happened, Patsy had given birth to the fifth, now fourth child, and it and the three others went to live with Grandma Sis and Screwball, taking the seven or eight kids they still had at home back up to about a dozen, but Marvin's kids were the youngest and Sis raised them as if they were her own.

Sis was a good woman. Nobody ever said a bad word about Sis.

But Screwball was not a good man.

He never worked much and when he did he was a prison guard. One might suppose that a man like The Screw might have found an outlet for sexual deviancy there, or perhaps he enjoyed watching the sadistic treatment we hear now was the norm in southern chain gangs at the time. But that would only be speculation.

The Screw subsisted on a diet of Cocolas, Goody Powders and Paregoric when Goody Powders and Paregoric were still full of dope. He was always sick with something and he needed it. He'd open one of those little glassine packs of Goody's and tip it into the Cocola and shake it up and drink it down in one swallow and that

17

would get him by for an hour or two, with enough Lucky Strikes in between.

Screw raised hogs, or at least he oversaw the kids as they raised the hogs. Hogs have to be fed. So Screwball would go to the welfare office once a month and get food, which is what you did before food stamps, and which mostly only colored people would do because the rest of us had pride and nobody with pride would go to the welfare office.

It came in sacks. Sacks of flour and grits, and heavy brown paper bags full of powdered milk, which nobody would drink because it tasted nasty.

And the more kids you had the more sacks you could get. There was no paperwork to fill out, couldn't have filled it out anyway, just show them the kids. They counted the kids and gave you the sacks. Screw always took Marvin's kids along to get his sacks since they looked so pitiful and like they couldn't help it.

Hogs have to be fed, and hogs like flour and grits. And hogs especially like powered milk.

Nobody thought it was right.

It wasn't right to go to the welfare office to begin with.

It wasn't right to get those free sacks of food.

And it wasn't right to slop it all to the hogs. At least that's what those of us who had pride thought.

Screwball didn't care. Prideful or not, he always had a sausage patty which the rest of us didn't.

Patsy's oldest girl grew up to become a whore at the truck stops on the north side of Charlotte and her sister followed her when she too came of age, working at the topless joints that used to run all along I-85 to Gastonia.

People knew the girls were in those places even though they would never go in to those places themselves but they knew other people who had been in there, people who would sometimes go in there by mistake or who knew somebody who had heard about somebody else who had been there and they came back and told about it.

The boy who was the next to the last one did okay, drove a truck, got married, had kids, always a quiet, gentle man.

The youngest, the one who Patsy was pregnant with at the time, her name might have been Janice, well she ran off and disappeared. It was said that she might have gone to Florida to be with her mamma but that was just speculation, wishful thinking at best. Most likely, she just ran off and then she disappeared. Girls disappear.

Karma bit Screwball in the ass real hard.

Sis died before him. He couldn't take care of himself in the best of times and he got sugar diabetes and they had to cut off both his legs so he was in a wheel chair and living with his oldest girl, Betty Jean.

Betty Jean took him in in return for the inheritance, which was five acres of next to nothing and couldn't have been worth the trouble, but we take care of our own. After the diabetes, he got something else that ate away at him causing him to lose some of his ear and part of his nose. It was most probably just the diabetes getting bad but the nose part sounds sort of like syphilis.

In the end, it was most likely the two packs of Lucky

Strikes a day that finally got him. He had just rotted away, what little there was left.

I heard about the funeral but didn't go.

ॐ

Me and Poor Tilly

IN THE SECOND GRADE, OLD LADY PRUITT, a vile, ugly, simple-minded, bull of a woman put Tilly Hartsell on display in front of the class.

She explained to us what it meant to be *pooh-ah*. (Perhaps dropping the 'r' lent a certain aristocracy to the issue, an aural reinforcement of our noblesse oblige in dealing with those less fortunate than ourselves.) It was because she was *pooh-ah* that Tilly always wore the same dirty dress, never washed or had underwear or shoes. Don't doubt it for a minute, in John F. Kennedy's America, poor kids came to school barefoot and half naked. At least until something could be done about them. And the rule in second grade was either up or out, after all, this was the greatest country in the world.

And because we all loved Tilly so, and understood her plight, Miss Pruitt decided to have Peg Lambert, the woman who cleaned out the trash cans and mopped out the bathrooms, come and get her and take her over to the high school gymnasium and clean her up, stick her in the shower, mop her down, wash her clothes and bring her back in time for lunch.

I had never been in a gymnasium, wasn't sure what it was. Nor had I ever seen or taken a shower. But I had the concept.

Once scrubbed, with clean white cotton panties,

second hand shoes and her old dress freshly washed but not yet completely dry, as was her hair, Tilly was put up in front of the class again so that we could all dutifully applaud enthusiastically, if not sarcastically, at the New and Improved Tilly Hartsell.

Her humiliation was complete. Good intentions gone awry.

The next day, she showed up like she always had, shoeless with a fresh coat of dirt from head to toe but panties intact. We checked to see.

The day after that, she appeared not at all, never again.

Was she ungrateful?

Or had Old Lady Pruitt exacted her simple minded revenge in the guise of removing bad influences from the group, one bad apple gone, the bushel saved, take the cure or get out, one chance at salvation and that's it? I was too young to know, too young to care. Tilly was a blip and the blip was off my screen.

[Fast forward eight or nine years]

On the other hand, Tommy Wylie was a champion.

Tommy Wylie drove a Volkswagen Beetle. A Bug. It wasn't his, belonged to his daddy and it was the only bug in town and a somewhat incongruous car for Tommy to be driving since he was captain of the football team and captain of the baseball team and an all round track star, on top of being ambidextrous and muscular, with oddly thinning hair which made him close to bald before most of us had started to shave. He should have driven at least a Ford Fairlane. A Galaxy 500 Fastback was what he aspired to, so he could practice up on his stock car racing skills, him the new Fireball Roberts.

The guys who never had any intention of graduating mostly worked second shift in the mill and they all had new cars, big fast cars, since their mammas and daddies worked in the mill and made regular money and could cosign the loan. Not good money, but regular money and regular was better than most. Regular money was what you needed to buy stuff on time.

Tommy had been sexually precocious, physically, hormonally, even back in the lower grades. At ten years old, he was already Charles Atlas, muscular, with thick pubic hair, heavy balls and an eight inch cock. I know because somebody had took a snapshot of him naked and he was passing it around on the school bus. You couldn't get by with that sort of thing now, but then, no harm done. Everybody was envious, boys and girls.

Tommy was destined to become one of the world's great athletes, at least according to Coach Ray. He could throw right or left-handed, had a lightning fast ball, a blistering hundred yard dash, a near-record long jump. And, with the total absence of any sense of pain, a football scholarship had to be just around the corner, which he would take and become famous before moving on to his race car driving career. Tommy was a man with a plan.

It was Tommy we all looked up to and admired, the man who would speed away, leaving us all in his NASCAR dust. As is so often the case, it didn't quite work out that way. He ran his own, small office cleaning business, dead at fifty from bad cancer, deep faith in Jehovah, no treatment, too far gone anyway. A shame.

(Never tell God you have a plan.)

[Back to Tilly]

So it was Friday night and Tommy and his buddy Larry and my friend John and me were parked behind Lowder's Service Station on Highway 49 and Cold Springs Road, about 11 o'clock at night, drinking beer and talking pussy, when a piece of shit 1962 Pontiac Catalina slid up. The door opened, something fell out and the Pontiac drove off. Never saw who was driving.

What fell out was Tilly Hartsell. Hadn't changed a bit.

It took a minute for her to get her bearings, like one of those Arabs dumped in the desert who just had their hood snatched off.

You could hear the silence as we collectively sized each other up, wondering who would speak first.

It was Tilly. "I've got to pith."

I'd learned that Tilly was tongue-tied back in the second grade, a few weeks before she had simply vanished.

Tilly was tongue-tied, as were many of the kids in class due to a variety of ailments, physical, mental, and social.

At the time, I was sitting in the back of the class with Buster the Crayon Hustler when this tall, dark, very attractive woman who you could tell wasn't from Mt. Pleasant just by the way she was dressed, came into the room, suddenly, unannounced. She and Miss Pruitt whispered and nodded to each other, and then whispered and nodded some more.

Miss Pruitt started pointing and calling out names.

Just the names.

No instructions.

Just the names.

Point.

Homer Edwin.

Point.

Jerry Weiss.

Point.

Tilly Hartsell.

Point.

Shirley Humphries.

Point, point.

The Goode boys.

By now, the rest of us were snickering, realizing that she was pointing out all the dummies, the stupid kids, the retards, each of them with speech impediments like Tilly. And when she named the Goode boys, brothers in the same class because the one with the cleft palette had already flunked a grade, we knew for sure the direction this was heading.

Pregnant pause.

Whispers between the bull and the beauty up front, giggling amongst us, the above average boys and girls.

Silence among the chosen few.

In the front of the class, they were nodding in agreement. Maybe—one—more?

Old Lady Pruitt raised her arm so that she could reach above the heads of all the other children and point all the way back to the back row.

Point.

And Coon, no *Con*-ley, Conley Boyce.

We were all supposed to follow Misses Swaringen

down the hall.

It didn't make sense. I got to tell you, it scared me. Scared me good. I had never stood in line with retards before but I had seen the prisoners at the camp down the street from where we lived do it all the time. I asked my daddy why they always had to stand in line, what they were standing in line for, what was going to happen when they got inside the building. He told me they were standing in line to get a ass whuppin. I believed him. Come to think of it, he was probably right.

We walked single file, bolt upright, quiet as the walking dead behind tall, dark, svelte Misses Swaringen into the room beside the principal's office, the room where they said you went in and never came out, a death march, me and the misfits.

Inside, there was:

A table.

A bare, hundred-watt bulb hanging down from the ceiling.

A dozen chairs.

Nothing on the wall.

No posters.

No blackboard.

No alphabet, cursive or otherwise.

Just the table and chairs, all set up for interrogation.

Mystery woman reached up and pulled a cord that hung down from the ceiling. A bright light glared down on a box and a deck of cards.

There was Tilly, and Shirley, and Homer, and Jerry, and me, and then the Goode boys sitting at the table side by side.

No way, no way in hell I'm supposed to be here.

Misses Swaringen explained that we were going to learn to play Go Fish, which was a simple enough game but it took a while to get the idea across considering the group, although I thought I had it figured out early on. Misses Swaringen said it was okay if we really didn't know how to play since we weren't keeping score, just look at a card and ask the person to the right—this is our right hand, this is our left hand—spatial geometry part of the lesson—for a card and say what it is.

"Okay? Ready?"

Misses Swaringen pushed a button on the box sitting in the middle of the table and the wheels on the top of it spun in unison.

"Tilly, ask me for a card."

"Thdo thu haf eny ates?"

"Go fish."

"Now Shirley, ask Tilly for a card."

"Wo you got trees?"

Yes, Tilly had trees and Misses Swaringen showed her how to give them up, even though Tilly Hartsell didn't want to give Shirley Humphries a goddamned thing.

Jerry got by okay.

Homer, my requestee, was severely learning disabled with one bushy eyebrow and front teeth that overlapped. I inquired, "Homer, wonder if you'd have a nine, old boy?"

"Glue, glue, glue, glue, glue."

Misses Swaringen reached into Homer's hand and pulled out a nine.

Not a problem for the Goode boys. I think they had

played this game before.

Done. Game over. First round, anyway.

Misses Swaringen pushed the button like before and the wheels spun backwards now, fast, and stopped with a loud snap, which made us all jump and scared Homer to the point of tears. The Goode boys slapped the table in imitation of the sound and Misses Swaringen told them not to do that.

She was pretty. Real pretty. Tall, with dark black hair, red lipstick, red nail polish, a kind of tight fitting skirt with a loose fitting cream colored blouse under a tailored jacket that had big lapels with thick piping and fabric buttons in a contrasting color. Chanel? Might have been Coco Chanel, I thought to myself.

Snap! She pushed the buttons again and the Goode boys slapped the table again even louder this time and she told them not to do that again.

"Now listen," she said.

Tilly said, "Thdo thu hav eny ates?"

No! It was the box. The box said, asked rather, "Thdo thu hav eny ates?"

It sounded just like Tilly.

Un-fricking believable.

The box, which also did a perfect imitation of Shirley Humphries said, "Wo you got trees?"

Magic, sheer magic, how did it work? The box with the wheels on top was talking just like them.

Box Jerry did a passable request for fives.

Next, "Romer, do you have a rine?"

"Glue, glue, glue, glue, glue," from Box Homer.

Stop!

Go back.

I played it in my head.

"Glue, glue, glue, glue, glue."

No, before that.

"Romer, do you have a rine?"

"Romer? Do you have a rine???"

Not my voice.

The box had skipped me.

I listened for me, waiting for the box to catch up, playing that last comment over and over in my head, "Romer, do you have a rine?"

A rine? Romer?

I was one of them.

Time stood still.

The rest of that dumb-assed game was just a blur.

I said it again to myself, again in my head, "Homer, might I have a nine?"

I listened carefully as I spoke the words, syllable by syllable.

My diction was perfect.

My accent proper.

But The Box. The Box was lying. It had to be.

But by now I knew, The Box didn't lie. The evidence was true. I had to redeem myself. I had to escape this Kafkaesque hell I had unwillingly and unwittingly been cast in to.

I reached over to push the button and take control but Beauty slapped my hand. Gently.

What could I do for her? What would entice her to let me push her buttons, perchance to end this charade?

No chance. Time was up. Session finished.

(Since then, I've learned to simply put $150.00 on the table on the way out and schedule another appointment for the same time next week, but that's another story, another day.)

She sent them away, all of them back to where they had come from, back to suffer through their miserable little lives, destined always to be below average.

It was just her and me now, alone in the room together.

She must have a soft spot upon which we could relate, if only I could find it. I traced a line starting under her hair, from the back of her ear, across the nape of her neck and down the lapels which ended in a V just where her cleavage began and her breasts rested, perceptible under her silk blouse only in my imagination.

She took me in her arms.

Her pheromones were intensifying by the second.

She told me there was nothing to fear, that I had performed fine. She told me I was still above average. I was not one of them, nor would I ever be. I was special. I would never have to come back to this room again—not if I promised to do exactly as she told me. But I must keep my promise. I must subjugate myself to her will, I must be a big boy whom she can trust and depend on always to do what she says.

I was.

I am.

I always have been.

She told me to watch TV.

Listen to what they say.

Listen to exactly how they say it.

Listen to the sound outside, not the sound *inside*, my head.

After they say it, you say it too, she said. Out loud. Right after they say it, you say it too. Just like them.

Practice. Practice until you sound just like them.

She caressed my head against her breast, the vent between her bosoms channeling her fragrance right into my soul. I had found my master. She tapped me on the head with her magic wand and bid me return to my world, my drab, gray world, never to see her again, except in my dreams.

And so I learned that the rain in Spain does fall mainly on the plain, and that nothing will get your clothes Cleaner! Brighter! Whiter! than new Duz in the Money Saving 64 Ounce Box available at fine supermarkets everywhere. I saw the U.S.A. in my Chevrolet.

Over the years, I spent countless hours sitting on the floor staring up at the TV in rapt attention, to learn from the masters, Johnny Carson, Monty Hall, Bob Barker, my apprenticeship in the world of peddling shit to suckers off to a flying start.

[It's after the commercial break, Segment 2 at Lowder's Store]

Anncr:

Ladies and gentlemen . . . welcome to our show this evening

And have we got an exciting show in store for you here behind Lowder's Gas and Lube

```
where Tongue-Tied Tilly is about to hike up
her skirt

spread her legs and tinkle tee all over the
back of our hero's car.

A big round of applause ladies and
gentlemen for tonight's guest star,

POOR — PATHETIC — PANTILESS TILLY HARVELL
FROM THE BACK SEAT OF NOWHWERE!

Tilly Girl — Come — On — Down!
```

"I've got to pith and I'm gonna pith on that Volksbug."

Over the years, I'd worked out that L sounds like N sounds like R sounds like W, Reekly Weeder thing, but Poor Tilly had not.

Why she wanted to pith on Tommy's car, nobody knew. She was probably just acting out to get attention. But it was our show and we had a celebrity performer and a hardened panel of judges so let's see what she could do—Pithing with the Stars.

On the one hand, nobody wanted to see her urinate, not really. But we did wonder if she would try, given that the back end of a Beetle is rather aggressively sloped without much to get a toehold on. Would she exceed our expectations? Would she give it a hundred and ten percent? Had she come out to play?

Pregame was finished. The team was on the field.

Tommy slapped a drum roll on the back fender.

With no encouragement from us, none whatsoever,

she backed up to the back of the Beetle. Bending slightly forward, she cautiously planted one naked foot halfway up the rear hood of the car. It stuck. A quick hop and the other foot was on. No need to stop now, she could grip the paint like a fly grips glass. She slid her left foot backwards until she could grasp the air vents with her toes and just as quickly entwined the toes of her right foot deep into the slots alongside it. You could tell from her fumbling that she had never climbed a Volkswagen before.

She started to crouch. In slow motion now . . . cautiously . . . shaky at the knees . . . she bent over, hiked up her cotton print dress, no panties to contend with, squatted some more . . . slowly . . . slowly, spread her knees just a little, thought about it . . . concentrating . . . her tongue between her teeth, her eyes closed, now a few drops . . . a few more . . . then a quick stream that stopped suddenly, then another, longer by a second or two, then a few more drops, which wet her feet and extinguished the traction between her soles and the high sheen from the fresh wax, which caused her feet to shoot forward whereupon she bounced ass first onto the asphalt.

It took her a few dazed moments to regain her composure, as it were.

"Shee-it," she said.

"Shee-it," we said, in unison. Game over. Home team wins.

We packed into the Bug and putt-putted away.

Did we suffer a crisis of conscience leaving Poor Tongue-Tied Tilly sitting there barefoot and pantiless in a puddle of warm urine?

No, we did not.

For even at that young age, we knew that Poor Tilly had nowhere to go, that, one way or the other, she was going to be wallowing in her own excrement for the rest of her life.

Me, I had mountains to climb, ads to write, shit to shill, maybe a life no so different after all.

Anncr:

Great show, ladies and gentlemen!

Be sure and join us next week when our guest will be . . .

♋

Me and Barking Dogs

WHEN YOU BEAT AN ANIMAL TO DEATH, you can hear the pleading in its voice. It is almost human.

When you tie a dog by its front paws so that it is hanging just an inch or two off the ground and then beat it with a belt or a piece of cable the size of a pencil lead, it doesn't just howl, it begs. It cries. And just before it dies, it moans, almost weeping, breathless from crying, like a baby's whimper.

I know because I've heard it. And seen it. More than once.

To be fair, my father didn't always beat them to death. More often than not, when they quit howling, he'd cut them down and drag them off and shoot them. But it was about the same either way.

A lot of people liked my dad. He did them lots of favors, fixing their motors and telling them old timey down home stories. He just hated a dog that didn't do what it was supposed to do.

He was a lot like that with his family.

That story is not mine alone. It has been recited thousands of times, common as dirt.

But no matter how many times you've heard the story, it is not the same as hearing the dog howl.

ᘯ

Me and Junior, Jr.

JOHN, GOOD, BROWN, JAYBIRD AND MUTT. Those were the names of my mother's brothers.

Only those weren't their real names, except for John.

Their real names were John, D.W., M.B., J.V., and J.R.

Why only initials? I'm not sure. It was probably just a case of, in the depression era all the big shots in the movies and the captains of industry and such, were known by their initials.

As in, "Gotcha Chief. I'll get right on it J.B.!"

Or, "Whatever you say, J.B."

D.W., M.B., J.V., and J.R. them was high society names, names a man could live up to. There was no great depression in the house where J.B. lived. That's my theory anyway.

In his younger years, Jaybird was also known as Crowbar, since his member had a sharp bend to the left—or was it to the right?—but a sharp bend no matter which way you looked at it. It got that way either when a horse stepped on it or a cow bit it depending on who was telling the story. The cow bite scenario always made the most sense to me.

Crowbar Jaybird J.V. Whitley, deep in debt, working two shifts at the mill, gassed himself in his car, laying in the back seat with a hosepipe stuck in the exhaust and the engine running, as was the fashion of the day. The casket wasn't opened because, "since he had laid in there all night before they found him the next morning when he didn't show up for work, he had done swold up and was plum black."

Everybody liked Jaybird. He was married to a woman named Jayvee. (No, I'm not kidding and I'm not making it up. J.V. was married to Jayvee and yes, I know there had to be something behind that J.V.-Jayvee thing but I never heard and I to this day don't know what it was, probably just teenage serendipity.) Everybody liked Jayvee too—except for a couple of J.V.'s sisters who blamed Jayvee for J.V. killing himself. Somebody always has to be the blame no matter what and it's usually somebody else that takes the rap. But Jayvee loved him for sure and she grieved him until she herself died, fifty years later.

Brown-M.B. was told that he could not be in the army without a real name and since he was standing in line to join World War II he had five minutes to pick one, do it quick. Matthew Braddus, it was, called Brad by his wife Estelle and no one else.

Good? He was okay.

Mutt was Mutt and comfortable with it. As a young man, he did a year and a day in the federal prison in Chillicothe, Ohio for making liquor, which, according to him was only for personal consumption while laying up in the woods with a bunch of ole girls who just wanted to lay up and have a good time, but it was illegal and the Law was the Law and Uncle Mutt was just one more of hundreds of thousands of victims of the War on Drugs, Back Then.

Mutt settled down to slopping his hogs in the morning, cutting hay in the afternoon and working third shift in the cotton mill to pay for it since there was no money in hogs or hay. No money in the mill either, nonunion, but that was what you did when you had nothing else to do.

After two daughters, Lilu and Doodle, he named his lastborn, lastborn legitimate anyway, a son, not Mutt, but J.R., a tip of the hat to tradition and the respectability he could never have, since a year at Chillicothe marked you for life, even in a place where half your neighbors had done time for something, either stomping somebody's ass or more likely making liquor.

The boy was christened J.R. Whitley, Jr. There's a symmetry to the name which I'm sure was lost on everybody at the time.

J.R. Whitley, Jr. was called Junior for short.

Progressive educational thinking during the Lyndon Baines Johnson years was that children should all write with their right hand and never their left—*right*-hand, *write*-hand, *right*-handed, *right*-hand-to-*write*-with—and not have nicknames.

Which presented a problem for Junior.

Teacher asked him his name. He said Junior.

She said, not your nick name, your real name. He said Junior. So she said, tomorrow, when you come back to this classroom, I want you to know your real name. Let us assume she wanted to know what the J and the R stood for, not able to allow that they might stand for nothing at all, or more likely just to show her own cultural superiority to the hicks she had to teach, her preferred techniques being ridicule and distain.

Next day, same question. What's your name?

Junior said with obvious pride in absolutely knowing for sure the only thing in life he knew absolutely for sure, "My name is J.R. Whitley, Jr. *Junior.*"

She took a paddle to his ass, hard, which caused him to shit his pants, thereby falling out of her favor once and for all. He was sent to the principal's office for not knowing his name and shitting his pants. Thanks be to God he was not left handed.

Episodes like that can taint a person for life and Junior, Jr. tainted bad. Eight years later, Miss Littaker, the schoolteacher, got knocked upside the back of the head with a two by four as she was walking up the steps to the front door of her apartment in Concord. Being a Christian Lady, with only love in her heart, she surely went to heaven where she occupied one of the many rooms our father has made for us in his mansion. (I've often wondered, if there is a God, does he put her in solitary confinement in that magnificent mansion, or does she get to share it with others like herself?)

She went to heaven. Junior, Jr. went to jail, a menace to society. A few thought it was a fair trade. Others didn't because we can't have innocent old ladies knocked in the head on their front door step, and society wasn't to blame, no matter what them eggheads said about crime in comic books and shoot 'em up westerns on TV because we make our own decisions in life, no matter whether you were born with good sense or not.

Justice must be done.

It rarely is.

CR

Me and God's Creatures

I WORKED AT K-MART.

In the feminine hygiene department.

It's where I saw my first waterhead.

And where I fell in love with Naomi Blizzard.

It was at the far end of Freedom Drive, which is to say on the outskirts of Charlotte. It was a new K-mart and the location matters because after you crossed I-85 to the north, a hundred yards away, you were in the country. And the country people who lived on the other side of I-85 would come in in droves to buy Kotex.

It was always a man driving, usually a pickup truck but a lot of times they'd be hauling a flat bed trailer. At the least, they'd bring a station wagon.

A single Kotex was half the size of a roll of paper towels, so a carton full of them took up a lot of space, and K-Mart sold them by the jumbo case as a loss leader. One case was half the size of a refrigerator and the country people wouldn't leave without 6 or 8 cases, sometimes 10 or 20 strapped down to their trailers or on the back of their trucks, or cinched down with twine on the tops of their cars.

It was a full time job on a Saturday for me and Naomi to roll them out by the pallet load after the K-Mart shoppers went through the checkout and paid and got a slip of paper for how many cases they'd bought.

'Stock boy from Aisle 12 to the checkout,' was the secret code that told us that somebody had bought too many cases to handle all by themselves, so we'd haul them out to the parking lot and load them up.

Naomi was swarthy, with dark, curly, kinky hair over all of her body except for the parts that showed. Not Ewok hairy, but still hairy, with hair that ran from under her arms, got a little thin as it ran down her sides but picked up again, thick and fluffy across her hips and inside her butt cheeks and between her legs, completely covering her belly and down her thighs all the way to the tops of her knees where it ended abruptly where she shaved her legs.

Maybe she was Cajun.

She was an army brat and all army brats are borderline, one way or another.

Naomi was liberated.

Good looking, too.

Dark yellow-brown skin, crystal blue-white eyes, and hair, lots and lots of hair.

She always wore dark hose, the kind with the seam in the back, a tight skirt, zip up ankle boots and a long sleeve T-shirt with big, horizontal black and white strips, kind of French whoreish.

They'd unload the tractor trailers for us but we had to haul the boxes through the back of the storeroom and out into the feminine hygiene department which took up the better part of the wall on the far left side of the store.

As instructed, on Saturdays when they'd advertised then in the newspaper, we'd stack them as high as we could so that you could see them from anywhere in the store. Oddly, they never did do a blue light special. That would have been too vulgar. What we couldn't stack against the wall, we'd leave in the storeroom, which is where we drew our stock from when filling an order for multiple cases so as not to destroy our display out front.

Plus, if a woman came through and wanted only a single case—rare, but it happened—Naomi had to help her get in down and balance it across the top of her buggy, since it didn't look right for a man to interact with a woman during such a personal moment.

I was called aside and told as much by the feminine hygiene department manager, a short guy only a few years older than I named Jason. Jason felt it just didn't look right for me to be handling Kotex in the presence of women. Tying them down to the trailers outside, well that was fine, since ropes and knots were man's work, but under no circumstances should I ever speak to a woman while handling a case of Kotex. Jason was especially adamant about that since he was a general manager in training and knew the rules and regulations of K-Mart.

After a couple hours of hoisting those cases around—they weren't heavy, just cumbersome—Naomi would begin to perspire and start to walk funny, pinching and pulling at her tight skirt and doing a little half squat, like her legs were sticking together. And she got gamey.

I was working two jobs, one throwing newspapers in the morning and then coming in at ten when K-Mart opened and working a double shift when I could to save money to go to Turkey. I already had the plane ticket and had been advised that I would need at least $400 spending money for the ten weeks I planned to be gone and figured that my career at K-Mart needed to be about 200 hours long at two bucks an hour for me to make my nut.

I told Naomi of my plans. Big mistake. She wanted to go along but that wouldn't have worked out since I was going to spend time with my new wife who was already there and meet her folks in Izmir. I skipped the details, just said maybe, I'll see what I can do.

I had been at K-Mart a couple of weeks and was $200 to the good when we had a slow day which meant we had to haul all the Kotex cases that were out on the floor back to the storeroom—don't ask me why—but that was the K-Mart way, at least according to Jason who likely just wanted to throw his weight around, little dipshit that he was.

So Naomi and me propped open the swinging doors and I'm sliding the boxes through and she's stacking them back in the storeroom. I can hear her grunting on the other side.

I slide the last one through, un-chock the door and go back to help her finish up.

The light in the storeroom was dim compared to the bright vapor lights in the showroom and my first gist was that Naomi has just tossed the cases in a random pile, though that was not like her at all. Naomi was a neat, orderly person, her Army brat training in action. Once I got a good look at it, it wasn't random at all, more like a disjointed igloo, and Naomi was down on her hands and knees climbing through an opening at the bottom of the pile.

I took the bait.

As soon as I scooted inside and stood up, she slid a

case to close the door hole, hopped up on another case she had put in the middle of the little room she had constructed, lifted up her skirt and pulled her hose down to her ankles with her knees in the air and her butt hanging over the side.

I was hooked.

Hot, dark, wet and funky, with faint streams of light shining through the cracks between the boxes, reminiscent of heaven or hell, I wasn't sure which, though the fluorescent green mist that rose off Naomi made me think it was probably the later.

Jason walked through—you could recognize his footsteps—called my name and left through the swinging doors out to the Burger Chef across the street where he knew Naomi and I often took our break together, also against the rules since we weren't supposed to take our breaks at the same time.

I figured I'd better go after him, since I didn't want him to come back and discover our nook and caught up with him in the parking lot. He pointed to an old man and woman piling cases in the back of their beat up BelAir station wagon and told me to go help them.

It was dark outside but they were parked under a flood light and before I got up to them I noticed that it really was an old man and an old woman, which was odd since old people didn't come in to buy cases of Kotex. Usually it was a middle aged man and a woman with a couple of teenage girls who stayed in the car and never made eye contact.

We were down to one case that wouldn't fit in the back of the wagon so the man told me to go around to the passenger side and see if I couldn't shove it in the back seat.

I had to smash down the corners to get it through the back door but once I did, it slid across the vinyl seat covers. I'd shove it a couple of inches at a time until I had it all in.

By this time the old man had got in behind the wheel and his wife got in too and closed the front passenger door. As I slid myself out the back seat, a long, white hand with long, spindly fingers rolled over the seat back and into my field of vision. The fingernails were also long and beginning to curl under themselves as they do when they go months or years without being trimmed.

I followed the hand up a skeletal arm and was eye to eye with a waterhead sitting in the middle between the two of them.

I had heard of waterheads before. They weren't that uncommon I guess, but I'd never actually seen one, not face to face, just inches away.

My first reaction was fright, but as soon as it registered on me what it was, the waterhead smiled, a faint smile through thin lips, but a smile nonetheless. Her skin was so pale, so luminescent it glowed under the parking lot lights. Her oriental eyes curved upwards at the corners and her sunken, flat cheeks rose along with her lips, so that when she smiled the effect was one of a creature completely at peace, and that peace transferred itself to me so that I found myself not staring but gazing upon this odd visage, no pity, not shock, just pure awe and wonder.

I backed out slowly, the huge face and head coming

into full view, a halo from the glaring lights outlining the hairless dome of her head.

I think I smiled in return. I don't remember, but I hope I did.

Jason caught me at the front door, told me to tell Naomi that she had the rest of the night off and that I should spend the rest of my time policing up the storeroom.

I didn't know if Naomi would be there or not, but when I pushed the box inward to open the door to the cave and slide inside, she was still lying on her alter which had grown damp and begun to sag.

She pulled the T-shirt over her head, the beads of sweat glistening on the curly hair across her arms, between her breasts and across her belly, collecting in a puddle beneath the kinky curls, pooling in her navel.

I decided to pawn my camera for the last two hundred dollars and left for Turkey the same week.

My in-laws didn't really take a liking to me so I left Turkey gracefully and spent the next two months hitchhiking to London and back, catching the last charter flight of the season with two-dollars in foreign coins in my pocket.

I hitchhiked home from the airport, immediately got in my car—a Fiat 600 I'd paid $250 for—battery still charged—and drove back to the far side of Charlotte to the K-Mart.

She was gone.

C03

Me and the Terrorists at Starbucks, Part 1

I FIND THIS TROUBLESOME.

Dr. Sanjay Gupta was on CNN taking a tour of refugee camps, as he often does. This time it was the flood victims in Pakistan. He was crouched in a tent the size of a McMansion toilet with a dozen or so kids aged 6 to 12 huddled inside and he was doing a cutesy interview with two of the little girls, sisters, who were supposedly doing their homework. The oldest said she wanted to be a doctor when she grew up and asked Sanjay if she could practice her English with him. So Sanjay asked her name and what she wanted to be when she grew up.

And the little girl answered. In flawless English. In flawless freaking English.

It's not the cutesy, syrupy interviews that Sanjay specializes in that I find troublesome. What I find troublesome is that this child, sitting in a squalid tent, in a squalid refugee camp, without clean clothes or adequate food and water, with no home to return to, with no future that anyone can imagine at this point in time, this little girl speaks English better than half the eight year olds here in Pleasant Mountain, North Carolina.

May Allah bless that little girl for she and her sister are the future and the hope and the salvation of our planet.

Speaking of the Desert God in all his iterations, I was

in The Church of Jesus Starbucks in nearby Concord last week, where I worship regularly. (I'm sitting there right now as a matter of fact, writing Part 3 which you'll get to in a minute.) Go anywhere in Concord, stop somebody, look them in the eye and say, this place sucks, and odds are, they will rise to the challenge. They'll say, No-o-o. It used to suck, but not now, now we've got a St-a-a-r-B-u-u-c-k-s.

And a grand Starbucks it is. Built in a renovated Burger King, it's bigger than most, seats thirty people or more with a drive through that backs up all the way to the main road. It's—well, it's Starbucks—and it's the only Starbucks in town, proof positive that Concordites are hip and with it.

Go in any Sunday morning and you're likely to hear a bunch of 15 year old, wussy white boys from Concord First Assembly MegaChurch, wearing MegaDeath versus MegaJesus T-shirts, harmonizing to the delight of the caramel macchiato slurpers, bible thumpers, and Amway signer uppers, each of whom have a scheme or a scam and meet at Starbucks to practice their craft and peddle their wares.

It is truly a bless-ed thing to experience, praise be, Hallelujah.

In the Church of Jesus Starbucks, there's a group of old farts affectionately known by the baristas as the Suicide Club, which convenes most weekdays from nine until noon and every Sunday morning. The group is chaired by a socially conscious and politically progressive deep thinker named Mel who is attended to by a select few retirement-aged acolytes, mostly immigrants from

Phoenix and Portland and L.A., each desperate for the company of a like-minded soul and the opportunity to discuss whatever Chris Matthews and Rachel Maddow had to say last night. In Concord, you see, progressives are an endangered species who huddle in far corners and speak only in hushed tones. Liberal egg head types are viewed with overt suspicion, surely subversives intent on destroying Our Great American Way of Life. The gang hangs on his every word; Mel being a former flower child with a PhD in poly sci, turned druggy, turned dealer in Vegas, (*card* dealer in Vegas) who got laid off when the town went bust in the housing crisis. Now he's in Concord for reasons no one is quite sure of, where he lives in a small apartment within walking distance from The One and Only Starbucks, awaiting death from multiple maladies.

Although I'm not a bona fide member of the clique I occasionally join in. But truth be told, I mostly make a point of going by on Sundays because Mel buys the New York Times religiously, the only place in town you can get it and I go there to mooch what he's already read so that I don't have to pay for it myself. When you're flat broke six bucks is a lot of money just to follow SoHo rental prices and stay on top of what's happening on Broadway, guilty pleasures which I still enjoy but, alas, can no longer afford. I realize I can get it online for almost nothing, but I like the physical sensation of holding the world in my hands, snapping it and folding it until the broadsheet is a manageable quarter page as we commuters used to do on our daily grind on the Metro North from Greenwich into the City.

Mel would give me his leftover sections which I'd bring back to my house trailer (known by the locals as a single wide) and read while pretending to breakfast on croissants, Seville orange marmalade and Lapsang Souchong, instead of my usual boiled egg and white toast from the food bank.

The last time I stopped by our Venti Grande House of Worship, Mel was there in his preferred club chair which sits catty cornered to a worn-out leather couch. A new guy who was sitting on the couch across from him noticed that I had come to see The Man Himself and intuitively and politely slid down so that I could sit within mooching distance of Mel's throne.

Mel promptly leaned over and whispered to me, "He's a killer."

"What?"

"He's a killer. That guy is a killer," he whispered again.

Okay, well, everybody's got to be something. I turned to Killer and told him that I appreciated his letting me slide in on the couch.

"No problem man."

I felt an urge to bond.

He had a book in his lap, a Farsi textbook.

"Tough language, huh? Farsi's a tough language."

"It's Arabic, not Farsi," he says. "They're often confused. Farsi is Persian, Arabic is not. Persian is Indo-European. Arabic is Afro-Asiatic."

"Got ya. Still a tough language though, isn't it?" I had to say something to redeem myself while hiding my envy. Here's a guy, thirty, thirty-five years old, handsome, obviously well read, some kind of military background, give him a year or two and he's going to be pulling down $300k as a consultant to a defense contractor who has unlimited federal money to roam the earth bombing mud huts and killing goat herders.

I'm not eager to kill people for a living, but still, times are tough and you've got to go where the action is. For the United States of America, burning the skin off innocent children is the only growth industry left and not one for which we tend to hold people accountable. Plus, the training's free and the retirement's not bad.

He, the killer, had all the appropriate tattoos. Jagged stuff. Daggers and swords and barbed wire. Told me he had been with Blackwater. His last contract—his word, contract, not assignment—had been Afghanistan, which came on the heels of a two year stint in Iraq. He said he had left with a couple year's worth of salary in the bank and wanted to move into something with a more diplomatic bent.

"Why? Why not stay with Blackwater?" I asked. "They're a sound, solid mercenary organization. Great branding. Commanding market share. Leader in their class."

He said he had read 'The Shock Doctrine' by Naomi Klein, that it had been an eye opener and had changed his mind about U.S. foreign policy.

I told him I'd just finished it myself. No doubt, it's the seminal work on the economic motive for America's war—for which there is always an economic motive— and that I was glad to hear that he had rejected the whole Chicago-School-of-Economics-free-market-capitalism-thing and that I was eager to know how he planned to use his experience to spread peace and love and beauty throughout the emerging Arab world.

"So what about Iraq?" I asked. (Obama had just declared the end to combat, Mission Accomplished, Again.)

"Disaster. A cockup from day one."

I liked that 'cockup,' a decidedly English phrase, and wondered if he came across it 'in theater' or if it was an affectation to demonstrate his worldliness, an affliction that I, myself, occasionally suffer, though you could never tell it, I don't think.

"How about Afghanistan? In or out?"

"In. All the way."

"In! Why? For how long? What's to gain?"

"For as long as it takes," he says with learned confidence.

"And how long might that be?"

"Could be generations."

"Generations! So what's the plan? How do we achieve peace and stability in Afghanistan and still protect American interests, although I'm not sure America has any interests in Afghanistan?"

Turns out, he did have a plan, a well enumerated three part plan.

"First," he says, "we have to kill all the fighting age males."

"Kill all the fighting age males?"

"The whole culture is so corrupted and we've done so much harm there already that we can't leave until it's fixed or they'll just come after us, sooner or later. Anything less is a halfway measure. Only after we've killed all the young men, who are unsalvageable anyway, will there be any hope of changing the culture, building schools, modernizing the country."

I don't remember what Steps 2 and 3 were. I was too busy trying to wrap my head around that first one.

Kill all the fighting age males.

I gave him my email address and asked him to stay in touch. A little out there I thought but an interesting guy nonetheless.

I snatched the Book Review and the Style Section from the floor beside Mel's feet and left.

Kill all the fighting age males.
It's a plan, I guess.
Good as any.

CR

Me and the Terrorists at Starbucks, Part 2

Kill all the fighting age males.

I had a friend for thirty years. He was like a brother to me. His ex-wife and my ex-wife, the second one, had been best friends. Met him at his wedding. He was a Viet Nam vet. I was not. I drew a good lottery number, 288, never had to go. We grew apart, him and me, a friendship that just faded away. I hope he's doing well.

He lived in Gaffney, South Carolina, where he sold insurance and fixed-rate annuities to unsuspecting seniors, door to door.

[The next couple of paragraphs are a side trip I've included for color. They really don't have anything to do with terrorists at Starbucks but I can't think of Gaffney, South Carolina without being reminded of the Big Peach. And for me, it helps to set the landscape for what is to follow. But since it has no direct bearing on the narrative, I thought it might end up being misleading. But my editor, a good Baptist woman, said she liked it, thought it was the best part of the whole book. So I thought, well, if she got off on it, maybe you would too. I just don't know. I've struggled with it and still can't figure out what to do. In or out? So, I decided to let you decide. If you want to read it, please do. If not, just skip to the next break in the text and pick it up from there. CJB]

In Gaffney, there's a water tank called The Peachoid. It's the Eiffel Tower of South Carolina. And it does look just like a giant peach, with a most subtle neoimpressionist paintjob that blends the yellows and oranges and reds, and yes, peach tones, in such a way that it indeed looks fuzzy. Imaginative idealization at its best, worthy of the Museum of Modern Art right there beside the Monet water lilies, if only it would fit.

But to the eye of most, the clefts of the engorged peach labia that merge gently into a prominent, red bud at the bottom of the tank resembles nothing if not a giant, fuzzy, upside-down twat. Take a woman, bend her over, stick a stem with a leaf on it in her butt and you get the idea.

[Street view it from Google Earth, see what you think. 35°05'42.74" N 81°41'09.11"W]

It is said that when it first sprung up, carloads of pubescent boys would pull over right there on I-85, especially on rainy nights, and abuse themselves while gazing upward towards the flood lit coochie, so close they could see the juices flowing down the luscious crevice and dripping off the bud. The local preachers were incensed, this monumental, 3-D icon of pornography having been erected in their midst, a temptation from no less than Satan himself. Personally, I side with the preacherman on this one, rare though it is that I share any point of view with disciples of Yahweh.

On the other hand, sometimes a peach is just a peach.

The controversy continues.

[If you skipped the Peachoid part, you can pick up the narrative here.]

My buddy in Gaffney had a small shrine to his service in Viet Nam on the dresser in his bedroom; his cap, medals, a teakwood carving of intertwined elephants that he had bought while on R&R in Thailand, and about a dozen Polaroid snapshots. I had glanced through them before but didn't see anything of note, never asked, didn't want to pry. They were photos of nothing, empty landscapes, bad photos I thought, by somebody who didn't know how to take a good picture.

I was hosting a small get together, catfish and Champagne by the pool at his place.

I'd taken a friend of mine, a much younger woman, Mary Ann, maybe 25, too young to remember Viet Nam firsthand.

Boldly, unexpectedly, she walked outside flipping through the Polaroids she'd found while prowling through his bedroom and asked him what was up with the pictures of nothing but empty jungle and river banks—exactly what I had wondered but never asked. (Pretty young women can get away with a lot.)

"What's this? These pictures? Nothing here. What's it all about?" she asked my buddy.

"You're not looking," he said. "Come over here by the light where you can see. See those little specks? Like little ants, you can see their legs sticking out? Those are people. I killed all those people."

Ants everywhere. I had never noticed them before.

"You killed them? Why?"

"Because that was what I was supposed to do. I was a

57

door gunner on a helicopter and door gunners on helicopters get to kill more people than anybody."

"All of them? Did you have to kill all of them?"

"Well, I didn't have to kill any of them, but why not? It's not like anybody cared."

"Wasn't it horrible?"

"No, it was Viet Nam. Viet Nam was the best time I've ever had in my life. I'd go back tomorrow if I could. I loved it there."

"You loved Viet Nam?"

"Sure."

"Killing all those people?"

He explained, "Most people have no idea how beautiful the place is. You get up in the morning, the sun's rising, the mist is lifting off the hills. You're in the air, taking guys out to the boonies where you're going to drop them off and then go back for them at the end of the day. It's a job. The daily commute. Most of the time, in the morning, nothing much happens. It's cool. It's clean. You're flying close to the ground. People are standing knee deep in rice paddies. Smoke rises from cook fires. Somebody driving a putt-putt hauls a load of weird looking vegetables down a dirt road. Kids chase each other around the hooches. Sometimes they look up and wave until somebody runs out to stop them. You drop your guys off, come back to base, do some bullshit duty, hang around until four or five o'clock, an hour or two before sundown. Then you go back to pick them up. But when you go back it's not the same. You get to the pickup zone and they've been shot up, wounded, maybe some of them killed. The gooks on the tree line are shooting at you so you get jacked up real high real fast. You can't see what you're shooting at, you just shoot back and get out as fast as you can. It's a huge adrenaline rush. You're pumped. You're pissed. Somebody you know is dead or wounded. Kill 'em all. If it moves you shoot it. Pity the poor fucker who's just hanging out on the river bank picking his nose watching a water buffalo take a crap. He's gone. *Tam biet mai mai.* Means goodbye forever. That's what they say."

"But you said they waved? Sometimes they waved to you?"

"Yeah, that was in the morning. Don't wave now motherfucker. Not now."

"Dead, just like that. You killed them just like that?"

"Just like that. So you get back at sundown and the new guys wash out the blood and body parts while you grab a tall one and the best hash in the world. You throw a steak on the fire, decide which baby love you want to screw and lay back. Maybe you spend two bucks for the pussy, fifty-cents for the hash. The rest is free, compliments of Uncle Sam. And the next day you get up and do it all over again. And after six months of that, day in, day out, what are you going to do for excitement when you get back stateside? Sell insurance? Viet Nam is a beautiful country. I love the place. I love the people. I'd go back tomorrow if I could."

Kill all the fighting age males.
Viet Nam.
Thank God we won.

[On the morning of March 16, 1968, United States Army soldiers murdered between 347 and 504 unarmed women, children (including babies), and elderly civilians in South Vietnam. Many were raped, beaten, and tortured. Some of the bodies were later found to be mutilated. Only Second Lieutenant William Calley, a platoon leader, was convicted. Found guilty of killing 22 villagers, he served only three and a half years under house arrest before being pardoned. He is still celebrated by some as a hero.]

ೞ

Me and the Terrorists at Starbucks, Part 3

[From press reports: On Nov. 19, 2005, U.S. Marines from Kilo Company, Third Battalion, First Marine Division killed 24 unarmed civilians in Haditha, Iraq, execution-style, in a three- to five-hour rampage. The dead included several children and elderly people, who were shot multiple times at close range while unarmed. One victim was a 76-year-old amputee in a wheelchair. A mother and child bent over as if in prayer were also among the fallen. "I pretended that I was dead when my brother's body fell on me and he was bleeding like a faucet," said Safa Younis Salim, a 13-year-old girl who survived by faking her death. Other victims included six children ranging in age from 1 to 14. Citing doctors at Haditha's hospital, The Washington Post reported, 'Most of the shots . . . were fired at such close range that they went through the bodies of the family members and plowed into walls or the floor.'

A few days after the story of The Haditha Massacre became public, U.S. forces killed 11 civilians after rounding them up in a room in a house near Balad, Iraq, handcuffing and shooting them. The victims ranged from a 75-year-old woman to a six-month-old child, and included three-year-olds and five-year-olds and three other women as well. A report by the U.S. military found no wrongdoing by the U.S. soldiers.]

Kill all the fighting age males.

One of these days, maybe—just maybe—a female in her late 20's or early 30's will stand in the middle of a major American city. Maybe in a big plaza. Maybe in a place where people congregate in the middle of the day, a place where they feel safe. Maybe not New York. Maybe not L.A. Chicago, maybe. Yes, let's pretend it's Chicago, but any major American city will do.

Maybe she will have a small thermonuclear device strapped to her body. Maybe she will have her finger on the switch. Maybe she will stand in front of a street-corner security camera. Or maybe she will set up her own video link on a cheap tripod with a live feed to the Internet.

Maybe she will speak into the camera and say, you killed my family. You plundered my country. You incited civil war. You destroyed everything that was good and made the bad even worse. For no good reason. And I am standing here now, for no reason other than that. So tell me America, why should I not share my experience with you? Give me a good reason and I will walk away. You've got 60 seconds.

And maybe the people on the street are watching themselves live on their iPhones. They know what is happening and even though they know they cannot run far enough or fast enough to escape the terrible blast that is one minute away, most will still run, screaming and flailing and ripping at their hair, just like the old ladies and mothers and children in a hundred Iraqi towns, when death, for no good reason, came to them.

[60 seconds]

Maybe a brave soul leans toward her, not wanting to get too close, wanting to stay far enough away so that the danger that is on her body cannot reach out and touch him. Maybe he will say: Yes, I know you feel bad, but, in balance, your country is better off now than it was before.

[50 seconds]

Maybe someone else will say: You don't understand. Most of us objected to the war. It's not *our* fault. You can't punish all of us for the actions of a few.

[40 seconds]

Maybe a woman will say: We are alike, you and me. You lost your family. I lost a son from a roadside bomb. Yes, he was in the military but he thought he was doing the right thing. He was serving his country. I know your grief. I share your pain.

[30 seconds]

Maybe another will try to make a rational appeal: It will be better. You just have to give it time. It takes time to establish a stable, western-style democracy. America went to war for you so that you could have the freedoms we have. Just wait. It will be worth it. You'll see. One day, where you live could be just like America.

[20 seconds]

From a young man, more desperate now: You let that trigger go and you know we will go back there and we will kill every man and woman and child, every dog and cat and monkey in that shit country of yours. We'll nuke it and pave it and you can take that to your fucking Muslim heaven.

[10 seconds]
You bitch. You rag-headed bitch.

Kill all the fighting age males.
It's a plan, I guess.
Good as any.

ଔ

Me, in a Blue Moon

I WAS SHOT DOWN AND LEFT FOR DEAD.

It was Friday about 6 o'clock at a bar in downtown Charlotte. Six o'clock on a Friday, early, hours before the usual crowd showed up to hear whatever jazz band was passing through town.

A place called the Blue Moon.

And in the Blue Moon, on that particular Friday at that early hour, there were only three people, me, the bartender, and a woman, a young woman, early 20's, freckles, red hair and just enough baby fat to be voluptuous, wearing a big flower print smock and a few drops of sweat which added a hint of musk to her peachy dime store fragrance. It was late July. Hot outside. Cool here in the dark.

One empty bar stool separated us.

What to say, what to say, what to say?

I knew the bartender, a girl named Day. She knew me. Had my glass of house Zin waiting. "Wassup?"

I told her I was waiting to meet Mary Ann, who she also knew.

Mary Ann was going to be back in town for the weekend catching up with an old friend of her own, Alex, so I decided to book a time slot for myself and treat her to dinner before a night of sex and make believe we care conversation.

Mary Ann had moved to the University of Virginia in Charlottesville, where she designed jewelry part time when she wasn't making designer pasta part time, something you can almost make a living at, part time, in Charlottesville. The intelligentsia likes its noodles and its jewelry to be both artsy and handmade.

Mary Ann had told me that she was planning to spend the afternoon with her friend Alex, because, well, because when Alex is available, one always spends the afternoon, or whatever time Alex can allow, with Alex. It was obviously a privilege, though I was not sure the nature of the treat. I didn't ask any questions, as is my nature. I am not an inquisitive person as a rule.

And at this point I didn't mind one little bit because I was looking forward to spending the meantime with Babealicious, one barstool away.

What to say, what to say, what to say?

I was working on it and when I figured it out, I knew it was going to be good but it hadn't come to me yet. I didn't want to be too bold, too forward, because Baby Doll was a delicate creature, worth taking the time to get it right before making my big move, deliver my suave line.

What to say, what to say, what to say?

The blacked-out front door swung open, the sun blasted through and in walked James Dean. Five-foot four, ninety-pounds, tight as a tick in black chinos, Doc Martens, hair parted hard with a wide-toothed comb slicked back with Vitalis, a white T-shirt with a pack of Marlboros rolled up in the left sleeve and a set of picture perfect little A-cups with razor sharp nipples poking out of the cotton pinched tight around her chest.

Without missing a step, she sashayed over and plopped her skinny little ass dead center of the bar stool that separated me from My Girl.

"PBR," she said to the bartender.

She looked at me.

I looked at her.

I looked at the bartender.

The bartender looked at her.

She looked back at me.

In the back of my mind, I could hear that theme song, the one from 'The Good, the Bad and the Ugly' that whistle they played every time Clint Eastwood or Lee Van Cleef would stare somebody down.

[I'm sure you know it but in case it's not ringing a bell, click http://en.wikipedia.org/wiki/File:Ennio_Morricone-The_Good,_The_Bad_And_The_Ugly.ogg]

James Dean sucked down half the Pabst Blue Ribbon, both elbows on the bar, put the bottle down just loud enough to make a point, and eyeballed the girl up and down.

Then me, up and down.

She took a suck off her beer.

I sipped my Zinfandel.

"Hey, what's your name?"

She was not talking to me.

"Che-e-e-ri."

"Cheri. That's a pretty name."

Giggle, giggle.

"And Cheri, you're a pretty girl."

"No I'm not."

"Yes you are."

"No I'm not, nobody ever tells me I'm pretty."

Whereupon James Dean grabbed her by the hips, swung her around on the barstool until they were face to face, eye to eye, wrapped her legs around the girl's waist, now all but sitting in her lap and said, forcefully, directly, with no hint of ambiguity and a whole lot of Alabama drawl, "Darlin I don't care what those friends of yours say, YOU are a VISION to me."

Giggle, giggle, giggle.

A few whispers in the ear, a few more giggles, and the woman of my dreams was sliding off her barstool, weak in the knees, uneasy in her too high heels. James Dean steadied her, and arm in arm led her out the door.

Less than two minutes, start to finish, swear to God, they were gone.

I looked at Day, the bartender. "You know her?"

"Oh yeah. Sure do. Alex. She's good."

"You got that right."

"Didn't you say you were having dinner with Mary Ann?"

"Thought so. Maybe not. What'd I owe you?"

"On the house."

ભ

Me and Used Food

I WAS A FOODIE before Anthony Bourdain cooked up his first spoonful of black tar heroin.

I aspired to walk in the footsteps of Jacques Pépin back when, if any man around here cooked a meal other than boiling a pot of grits, it was a sure sign of ho-mo-sexuality.

On the other hand, I never whipped up a shank of Osso Buco with a side of spaetzle that didn't get me laid before the cheese course. Women love a man who can cook. Maybe only for one night at a time but that was okay too, it's good to switch up your dinner conversation, don't get yourself in a rut.

I used to approach romance abiding by Coon's Law, The 3 Things that will Never Fail to Get You Laid:

1. Cook her dinner
2. Take her skeet shooting
3. Let her fly your airplane

Them days is long gone and so much has changed that I don't even talk the same no more. Verb tenses are of no consequence here on Pleasant Mountain, NC.

With hard times I have developed a whole new appreciation for food, even the used stuff you get at the food banks. Not the cut or the marbling. Not the organic certification, or the free range stamp of approval, or the subtleties of preparation, or the blend of secret herbs and spices—but that it even exists. You have food, that's good. You don't have food, that's Bad. Bad's here. With a capital B.

So my cousin Junior lost his job on the loading dock. His unemployment run out and with his jail time never completely forgotten, there's not much chance he'll ever again find his place in a vibrant, growing American economy, one that can compete with the best the world has to offer, or some such bullshit. Bad is just another day for Junior Simply put, Junior's screwed. Me too.

So Junior went to the food bank in Albemarle where they told him that they were all but out of food, not much to choose from.

Junior said I'm hungry, I'll take whatever you got.

So they told him that all they had, meat-wise, was a bag of frozen pig tails.

Nobody else wanted them so he said I'll take 'em, cook me up some souse meat.

Didn't have no grits.

No cornmeal, can't make mush.

No black-eyed peas.

No beans, pintos or otherwise.

But they did have a ten pound sack of institutional muffin mix. Junior said he had ate a whole lot of institutional food while he was in the slammer and he'd take that too.

Being right before Thanksgiving, that holy day when we all sit down to give thanks to the Lord for all the blessings He has bestowed upon us, they had a couple cans of leftover cranberry jelly. Junior got him one.

The way I figure it, he can dip the pig tails in the institutional muffin mix and deep fry them like a corn dog and then glaze them with the cranberry jelly to add a little sparkle, a little zest.

Me, on the other hand, I'd make a pâté.

A lot of people don't eat souse meat, never heard of it, but if you put it in a little can, slap a Fortnum & Mason label on it, charge £6.20 for it, they'll stand in line to get some.

Marketing 101. You can sell anything if it's in a pretty enough package.

[Fortnum's is a great place to do your holiday shopping. Check them out at http://www.fortnumandmason.com We accept lover offerings.]

For those of you who sooner or later will find yourself in similar circumstances and want to add a little panache to the ass end of a hog, let me offer my recipe for Pig Tail Rillette:

3 pig tails

1 can of beer

1 carrot, peeled and chunked

1 celery rib, chunked

2 cloves garlic

5 cups beef broth

1 shallot, finely diced

1 tablespoon whole grain mustard

Dash of hot sauce (optional)

5 sprigs of fresh thyme, finely chopped

Salt and course ground pepper

Maybe a little fresh lemon juice if you have it

Dump the pig tails in a cast iron pot with the carrot, celery, onion, garlic and a can of beer with enough water, if necessary, to cover the tails.

Cook it all for most of the day until the meat is falling off the bone.

Let it cool down and dredge the fat off the top.

Put the meat in a food processer and shred it, not too fine at first.

Put in everything else and blend it until it begins to take on the least bit of air.

Fold in the liquid fat you skimmed off the top until it has a creamy consistency.

Put it in the refrigerator overnight.

It'll keep—so you can eat on it for a while.

A Frenchman might eat it on a baguette. I like toast points myself. Pepperidge Farms white bread works just fine and you can sometimes get it at the food bank in Mt. Pleasant, which tends to have a better selection than the one in Albemarle.

Innovation. That's the American way, taking responsibility for our own selves and getting by with what we got and not looking to the government to give us a free ride for this mess we got our own selves in and only

have our own selves to blame for.
    Bon appetite!

ௐ

Which Reminds Me

HOW ABOUT TAKING A MINUTE TO DONATE ten dollars to a food bank? Any food bank. Anywhere. It doesn't matter. Ten bucks. That's all.

Thanks.

Me and the KKK
and the Homecoming Queen

WHEN I WAS 15 OR 16, ME AND MY DADDY went to a Klan rally in the stubble field down at the end of the road between the prison camp and Highway 73. It's where I live now.

It was the 4th of July and George Wallace was running for President, a cause for celebration.

It was a big show. Klingons, Klutons, Klaxons and Klipshorns intent on saving Mt. Pleasant for the superior white race.

Who could argue with that?

According to them, we each shared a great heritage. We were one and the same, except that they were all wearing masks and I wasn't, and except too, maybe, that at that time the great white race in Cabarrus County, North Carolina consisted mostly of inbred degenerates worthy of a casting call for banjo pickers and sodomite extras in Deliverance. Who wouldn't envy their position in life and want to be just like them?

Big cross.

Big fire.

Big Jesus.

FBI agents doing their best to infiltrate the crowd but, No! No! No!, we knew who they were, which was anybody we'd never seen in town before. Anybody not wearing gallus overalls.

'Onward Christian Soldiers' was the first song I ever learned to sing by heart and they were singing it now. Watching these boys, I knew what it was all about, marching as to war, the cross of Jesus, the royal Master, Christ, leading us against the foe, the whole nine yards. Jesus himself was clearly on our side.

The show was almost over and it was time for the grand finale, the monumental burning cross, sure to strike fear in the hearts of any nigras who happened to be hiding in the bushes.

It fizzled, the Klingbot in charge having neglected to bring enough kerosene to properly soak the burlap sacks tied around telephone poles that were bolted together. (Just in case you ever wondered how they did that) After much heated discussion they all agreed that not one of them was dumb enough to strike the match to the gasoline someone had in the meantime siphoned from a Klanbubba's pickup truck. Contingency planning was not their strong point with nary an MBA in the bunch. However, dumb enough was not in short supply, with plenty of acolytes ready to sacrifice their eyebrows and maybe a little skin off their ass to the task of saving Our Sacred Southern Way of Life from the Communists Up North, whose hearts were set on infiltrating our Sacred Southern Soil yet again. No sir! Never again! Not tonight, anyway.

Kapoof! The cross was finally aflame, proof positive that, here on Pleasant Mountain at least, God's Will will be done.

I'd a figured the Konklave would have gone on all

night but me and daddy was home before the 11 o'clock news, which he thought would have Eyewitness coverage but apparently the Communist Controlled News Media decided otherwise.

Normally, my daddy would have been coon hunting at 11 o'clock at night, but, expecting to see himself on TV, he was planted in his recliner when the phone rang.

"Uh huh."

(Listen)

"Uh huh.

(Listen)

"Uh huh."

(Listen some more)

"Awright."

Come and look for Spud Banger's arm was what all the commotion was about.

He put his shoes back on and was out the door.

Of course me and my mamma and my sister all waited up until he got home a couple of hours later to see what was happening since the phone never rang after supper let alone 11 o'clock at night.

Turns out, a bunch of the Banger boys and some of their buddies stayed after the rally to throw some dynamite for the 4th. (For those of you who've never tossed a stick, it works like this: Cut the stick in half, put in a blasting cap with a six-inch fuse and hold it longer than anybody else, before chucking it as far and fast as you can.)

The objective had been to strike a decisive, if only metaphorical, blow in the Battle Against the Black African Race, who they knew for sure were conspiring right now on this Most Holy Fourth of July to creep into our sacred bedrooms and kill us in our sleep.

Winner is the man who holds on to it the longest. Or, in Spud's case, *loser* is the man who holds on to it the longest. Winner is the man who holds on to it *next* to longest. It was just one more of so many things they didn't quite understand.

It didn't go off as planned, no pun intended.

The Banger boy blew off his right arm, his ear, an eyeball and a couple fingers on what was left of his left hand. They called from the hospital and said that if you can find the pieces, maybe they can sew them back on.

Banger's buddies knew my daddy, being a coon hunter, had a twelve cell flashlight and wanted him to come and help look for the pieces.

As it was subsequently reported in the Concord Tribune, they found the pieces but instead of being big pieces they were bits and pieces. Banger was to live his life a maimed man, all because of the Hateful Negro.

At that same time, there was girl who sat behind me in French class named Sharon Barringer, a year older than me, big brown eyes, long brown hair and fair-sized breasts that seemed to always point right at you no matter which way she was turned.

So every morning at 10:30 I was turned around in my seat talking to her as she gently and carefully explained that although she enjoyed talking to someone like me, she could never actually date someone like me, someone who paid attention in French class and was a wiz in advanced biology—though in hindsight, those would seem to make me preeminently qualified as a bucket of fun back seat companion—because, as she enumerated carefully and slowly: a) I didn't even have a driver's license yet, and b) She had yet to date the entire football team and was running out of time in her quest to achieve adulation and recognition as the homecoming queen—although she didn't put it exactly like that.

She had me on both points, a) and b) though I thought a little flexibility on her part was in order as I tried to make my case logically, hoping to make up in brain power what I obviously lacked in sex appeal. As I learned then and have learned many times over in the years since, logic and love rarely walk hand in hand.

Sharon went on to become a kindergarten teacher and bear two daughters, all the while suffering a husband who wanted nothing more than the boat, the beach house, and to be rid of her.

After that, there was an almost-husband she didn't want to talk about — didn't want to think about — a man who was never a part of her life — or the lives of her children — a non-human being — an evil man — a despicable man — not really a man at all.

It had been a short-lived relationship.

After that, there had been an LTR with a doctoral candidate in philosophy fifteen-years her younger with whom, towards the end, she rarely spoke and never had sex with but he was a good companion and had once been fun to talk to but was now out of the picture except occasionally when he dropped by for dinner usually on holidays since he didn't have a family of his own and we felt sorry for him.

I was to learn all this whether I wanted to or not shortly after a chance encounter about a year ago in a quaint little bistro in downtown Charlotte where I was perched at a restaurant bar talking it up with a jewelry designer I'd just met, Mary Ann, the restaurant being named, appropriately, Carpe Diem.

Forty years, forty pounds, and two and a half husbands later and one whiff of me was all it took for Sharon Barringer, Eternal Homecoming Queen, to realize that her dream had finally come true. I was The Man from Somewhere Else.

"Bon jour!" exclaimed Sharon with unbridled exuberance.

"Hello," said I. "Long time no see."

That evening, afterwards in bed, wondering why I ever quit smoking, I noticed that faraway look of someone not totally in the moment. Was it me? Granted, I couldn't just pick her up and flip her around Kama Sutra style like I once imagined I could, but it was a reasonable performance on my part. So, like a fool I asked her if everything was all right.

"Was I that bad?"

"Non! Vous avez été superbe."

"Then why so sad?" I asked, with my left foot sweeping the floor, toes scrunching to snag my pants while pretending to pay her the post coital attention she thought she deserved.

"I was thinking about my cousin, Spodell. He was a class ahead of us in school. Well... he killed himself today, committed suicide. It was tragic. So sad."

"Why did he kill himself?" I asked, with one leg now

in my pants and the other foot searching for my shoes, making a point to maintain eye contact so as not to appear uninterested.

"Well... when he was just eighteen years old, he was at a Fourth of July celebration with friends and they were throwing dynamite and somebody played a joke on him and slipped him a short fuse and it went off too soon and it disfigured him. He lost an arm and an eye and ruined his testicles and for the rest of his life he was chronically depressed. All of his life he was just so, so sad. He never married, never had kids. Never enjoyed all that life has to offer. Sad. So today he killed himself, committed suicide and I just can't get over it. It is just so sad. Just so, so, sad."

"I remember hearing about that," I said.

I hiked up my pants.

"So, so, sad."

Tucked in my shirt.

Slipped on my shoes.

Felt my crotch.

Still had both my testicles. Time to go.

"So sad. Just so, so, sad."

"Bon soir, mon ami." I thought that was the way you said it, could have been wrong but I tried, the accent is really all that matters.

What I meant was good bye forever thank God never again.

"Call me?" she implored from her daze.

"Promise. Kiss kiss. Nite nite."

So sad. Just so, so sad.

Me and Mr. Vice President
of Kiss My Ass

TIMES ARE HARD AND I NEED A JOB and I'm not as picky as I once was.

I've got a friend who made a whole lot of money selling real estate in Florida before the big bust, specializing in what they called "Waterfront Properties" and indeed the properties were mostly on the water but in Florida water isn't hard to find. Just get yourself an old orange grove on an irrigation ditch and a couple of weeks with a bulldozer, bada bing bada boom, you've got prime waterfront property ready to be pre-sold to Cincinnatians, and Detroiters, and Clevelanders sick and tired of being left behind while everyone else is flipping lots and making real estate millions in their spare time like the ads they saw on TV.

So this friend of mine introduced me to the man who had been vice president of the whole operation, now looking for greener pastures, intent on leaving central Florida and all of those upset Cincinnatians with their wholly unwarranted lawsuits behind and moving on to the Greater Miami Metro Area. He had every intention of "dominating," his word, dominating, the south Florida market or he wasn't going to go at all, him being a master of the universe and all. And I could be a part of this domination, a team member with a ground floor opportunity alongside a proven mover and shaker. And the first step for us on that road to the total domination of greater Miami was to get to know each other a little better. Sniff each other's butts as they say in the world of moving and shaking.

Sounded good to me.

Mr. V.P. wanted to know what drove me, what my passions were, what made me get up out of bed every morning. He said the personal stuff was important. Said you can find a man who can do any job but you've got to look beyond the job and into the heart and soul of the man you're going to be working with.

Sounded good to me.

I told him my story, what defined me, what my passions, my dreams, my aspirations were. I told him I get out of bed each and every morning ready to seize the day, ready to grab it by the horns and beat the shit out of it until I have lifted every single penny out of Opportunity's pocket and put it into mine. No, ours. Our pocket. Maybe that was a better answer, lift every single penny out of Opportunity's pocket and put it into our pocket. Yes, it was, it was a better answer and I switched the thought seamlessly in mid-sentence, he never even noticed. I told him that I work hard, that I play hard, that I'm a team player and that, IMHO—in my humble opinion but I said IMHO to emphasize what an Internet savvy guy I really am—IMHO all that was holding me back was a mentor such as himself to guide me, to show me the way. Stand back, Miami! Hot damn, here we come!

Sounded good to him.

Then it was his turn to bare his soul.

Seems he was all upset after his mostly bimbo girlfriend had left him right after he'd paid a bunch of money to fly her to Los Angeles so that some famous nudie photographer could take half-naked pictures of her so that she could start her own "fitness" website.

Show her pecks and sell vitamins. A lot of girls do it.

He showed me pictures of her just like you'd see on cybergirl dot com, all hot and sticky from working out. She was huffing and puffing with big beads of artificial sweat on top of her waterproof makeup, all in soft focus, spreading her legs across some monkey bars in a gym, flexing those two muscles that run from your knees to the inside of your crotch, which, on her were very pronounced, ending behind a sliver of G-string. (You couldn't help but notice the stubble where her pubic hair should have been. It just seemed odd to me he'd pay for all that high dollar photography and not get her shaved up clean. That was the first inkling I had that Mr. Vice might not have been the brilliant organizer he presented himself to be.)

Truth be told, she wasn't that good looking. She was a little weak in the face. She did have real nice breasts though. He told me how much he had paid for them. I don't remember exactly, but it was a lot. He asked me if I noticed how they were just "faintly asymmetric" which made them look absolutely real. Said that was his idea, how to tell the pros from the amateurs when it came to boob jobs. Guess that was vice presidential level thinking. Never thought about it much but crooked breasts do look real, unless they're too crooked, which just looks like a bad boob job. The devil is in the details. They looked real, even close up, especially in soft focus. They were his breasts and he was justifiably proud of them. As I understand it, her job was to spend four hours a day in the gym plus two blow jobs. At least that was the story. But considering that she was in the twenty-four range and that Mr. V. was on the high side of fifty, my guess is it was more like two hummers a week and a lot of wishful thinking. Who knows, I could be wrong. There's always Viagra.

He spent the rest of the afternoon telling me what a brilliant real estate man he was, how he had been vice president of a company that flew retirees from Detroit and Cincinnati to Florida and convinced them that a five-thousand dollar lot was really worth three-hundred-thousand but today, and today only, he could get it for them for two-fifty with his own, exclusive, super deluxe financing package thrown in, satisfaction guaranteed or their money back, no questions asked.

I had no doubt it all was true.

Except after the bottom fell out a whole bunch of those proud new property owners decided they did indeed have questions to ask and wanted their money back, only to discover that they were shit out of luck. (Get rich quickers from up north should learn to read the fine print down south.)

Mr. V. went on to say that he owned a Jaguar but didn't drive it today, that's why he was in his old SUV, because he didn't have time to get the oil changed in the Jag and you know how those Jags are, they're real persnickety and if you don't get the oil changed when they say it's time to, well, hell, they will deem you an unworthy owner and refuse to take you anywhere until you do. Sort of like his ex-girlfriend. My guess is he didn't have the extra $39.95 to fork over to Jiffy Lube.

I thought he wanted me to do a job for him, talked to him for four or five hours. I still don't know what the job was, but it was something big for sure. Maybe that's why he didn't come right out and offer it to me; it was too big for someone like me who lacked that asymmetrical vice presidential mindset.

So when it was all over, my buddy asked, well, what do you think? And I said, well, he's a real nice guy considering he's a real estate salesman, and his real young ex-girlfriend sure did have nice titties, faintly asymmetrical and all, but I sure wouldn't want to buy swamp land from him, and I wouldn't make him Vice President of Kissing My Ass, in Miami or anyplace else.

Like I said, I didn't get the job.

Maybe next time.

ය

Me and My Type

I WAS HAVING LUNCH A WHILE BACK WITH BEATRICE, my fellow traveler through the underworld, and she asked me what was my favorite type. Like, what type of woman do you like best? She said "do you like" but what she really meant was "turns you on" as in, what type of woman turns you on, hint, hint, a woman like me—mid-fifties, not unattractive, bright, a good person to hang out with and, most of all, a good person to talk to. (Have you ever noticed that the older a woman gets, the more she wants to talk?)

I had to stop and think because I haven't thought about that in a while and things change and I wasn't sure what the answer was considering my new station in life.

And after I thought about it for a minute, I said, "A little pudgy. A little dykish. Tops on bottom. Twenty-two years old, with pierced labia and great big brown, oatmeal-cookie areolas. Short hair. Maybe a pink spike. Or purple. Yep, now that I think about it, that's the type of woman I'd like to spend some time with."

And Beatrice said, "But Coon, that's about as far from you as you can get."

And I said, "You know, that's exactly where I'd like to be."

ʘ

[An Update]

THE GUY FROM SANTA MONICA, the one who moved here to live with his childhood sweetheart because she had a job and he didn't—remember, she was a teacher, he was an actor, sort of—the guy that said that living around here was like living in a bucket of shit?

Sadly, it didn't work out.

She retired and moved in to live with either her son or daughter, I'm not sure which, I heard but don't remember, but anyway the son or daughter is a doctor married to a doctor so the couple is quite well off. They built a separate apartment for her in the back yard of their home in Myers Park, the old money neighborhood in Charlotte.

Thing is, they never had any intention of putting up with a used up actor for the next twenty years so he got the boot, ended up in a senior center in Asheville where he regales grayhairs with adventuresome stories of his days as an extra in Chevy commercials and the time he met Clint Eastwood standing by the catering truck, where he, Clint, ordered a hot dog all the way and a coke in a little bottle and ate in all in just two bites.

Oh well, so much for the subsidized life.

Once again, the arts, they do not pay.

CR

Me and the Man of My Dreams

THIRTY YEARS AGO, I MET A WOMAN WHO RAN a health food store. I had not seen her since until a while back when she was passing through and called to see if I could meet her for lunch at an old lady's white tablecloth restaurant in Asheboro, the sort of place that specializes in chicken salad on toast with a quarter head of iceberg lettuce smothered in Duke's mayonnaise.

She was buying. I couldn't say no.

She's done well for herself, quite well for herself, and comes back to North Carolina ever so often to see her family.

Maybe it was just the atmosphere of the place, or more likely her aristocracy compared to my whupped dog demeanor, when that Anthony Hopkins movie, *Remains of the Day* came up in our conversation, from out of nowhere, for reasons I don't remember.

(If you haven't seen it, it's one of those English mood movies. Anthony Hopkins plays a butler, loyal to the end, but with no life to show for it. Emma Thompson badgers him until she learns that he is, at heart, a dear, sweet, sensitive man who has spent his life in service to others, only to discover too late that the years have passed him by, his single and solitary pleasure being sappy romantic novels that remind him of the dreams he was never to realize, the life he was never to have.)

(Maybe now I do remember how this conversation got started.)

"Oh my God! That's it! That's you! You could be Anthony Hopkins! No, you *are* Anthony Hopkins."

"I don't understand."

"Anthony Hopkins. You could be just like Anthony Hopkins in *Remains of the Day*."

"Meaning?"

"Meaning, be a gentleman."

"I *am* a gentleman."

"Yeah, but sell it. Be a gentleman to rich old ladies."

"I don't know any rich old ladies—except you."

"Advertise. That's what you do, isn't it? You write ads. Write an ad."

I didn't particularly like the idea but being desperate I did what she said, thought I might turn it into a flyer and stick it on windshields down at the Shriners Club or post it on the Internet, Craigslist, maybe Christian Mingle, test the market, see what type of business I might drum up.

Here it is:

———— ‿ ————

The Services of a Gentleman

Well-spoken, well-read, reasonably well traveled

Published, with knowledge of, or experience in, fine art, classical music, financial services, international marketing

Computer and Internet literate

Licensed private pilot, though not current

Avid cook, gardener, bridge player

Casino savvy

Not fully conversational in French, German or Spanish, but can get by in a pinch

Tuxedo, Parachute

Experienced with firearms

Have each of Popular Mechanics '50 Tools Every Man Should Own' and know how to use them

Available for service as personal secretary, accompaniment for social occasions, or traveling companion

Open to suggestions from confident women of means

References

———— ‿ ————

I liked it.

Reasonable.

Understated.

True. Close enough, anyway.

But I didn't run it right away. I wanted to think it through, be prepared for the stampede from lonely hearts—each dreading yet another tour of the Continent alone—that I knew was sure to follow.

In the meantime, I was watching *Goldfinger* on my laptop, got the DVD from Netflix, the scene where Sean Connery is driving through Switzerland in the Aston Martin DB5. It opens with a trill from a harp, my favorite movie scene of all time. It is 1964. The Alps, clean, fresh, blue and green and beautiful. Wire wheels, knockoff hubcaps, bespoke suit, Walther PPK in the chamois holster under the left arm, ejection seat at the ready. The man I was always meant to be. And then and there I realized, I am not a whore.

Whatever I am, I am not a whore.

I am not a butler.

I am not an escort.

I am not a gigolo.

I am not a whore.

So I decided to mull it over. No need to make a hasty decision. I decided to surf for a paradigm, to see if there was a real life butler or escort or gigolo that I might not mind modeling myself after. (Market research)

Google delivers.

Once upon a time, when the world was learning to Cha-cha-chá and the Latin lover reigned supreme, there was a guy not unlike myself in a similar situation.

His name was Porfirio Rubirosa.

Doris Duke, the daughter of cigarette and electricity monopolies who inherited the current equivalent of $3 billion when she was twelve years old, gave him $500,000 back when a half a million bucks was real money, along with a stable of polo ponies, several sports cars, a B-25 bomber which had been converted into his very own personal aircraft, along with a 17th Century manse in Paris.

After which, he divorced her and kept the loot, chump change for her and a grubstake into the good life for him.

Next, he hooked up with Barbara Hutton from Woolworth Five and Dime money, the original 'poor little rich girl' who gave him *another* B-25 and a coffee plantation in the Dominican Republic along with $3.5 million as part of *her* divorce settlement.

The man was on a roll.

What was it? His charm? Good looks?

According to Truman Capote, with whom he reportedly shared some sort of intimacy, Porfi's charms were largely attributable to his eleven inch penis—erect, not flaccid, don't be ridiculous—in whose honor the long pepper mills you used to see in chichi restaurants in France were affectionately called Rubirosas.

Almost fifty and at the top of his game, Porfi last married a 19-year old French actress, got drunk after winning six chukkers of polo at the Coupe de France and drove his Ferrari at high speed into a tree on the way home.

The end.

Nothing wrong with that.

Okay, so what do Rubirosa and I have in common?

Some would say that he's a pepper grinder and I'm a salt shaker and that in the world of rich, lonely, loony old ladies, that can be the determining factor.

Maybe.

Maybe not.

But wait!

There's more.

Back to Google. Keyword [rich+looney+old+lady]

Zsa Zsa!

Zsa Zsa Gabor, to whom Porfirio was also romantically attached, had adopted her own sugar-baby. After being married umpteen times already, she took as her last husband a German Count. Count Arnheim von Beaujolais or something like that.

He had bought the title off a bankrupt genuine count, though it seems if you go belly up your claim to being royalty or landed gentry would, by default, automatically terminate. Apparently not.

And what were Count Whoever's qualifications prior to buying his title wholesale to impress the dickens out of not so über discriminating Zsa Zsa, thereby ensconcing himself as a demigod living high atop Mt. Beverly Hills? He was a hairdresser. A beautician. Curls and a blow dry.

[He has a cheesy website. http://www.princefrederic.com just in case you don't believe me.]

I can do curls and a blow dry, of sorts.

And I too live atop a Mt., of sorts.

And that thing about the salt shaker? That was just a

joke, me trying to be witty and self effacing at my own expense.

So now, I, too, am thinking heiress.

Maybe I can hook up with the Zsa Zsa of trailer parks.

Me, Count Coon von Concord, medals abreast.

She, Lady Merlene of Kannapolis, blond hair a-frizz, bosoms a-bouncing.

See us now, strolling into the Mayflower Fish Camp across from the Starbucks of Concord, the common people gawking and gasping and pointing—That's them, Count Coon and Lady Merlene!

In a town where the late Dale Earnhardt—famous around here for hard charging his NASCAR brains into a cement wall—warrants a genuine bronze statue in the middle of town, the love and admiration of the common folk is not that hard to garner, I do not think.

We'll see.

In the meantime, "Have Shaker Will Travel" reads the card of a man.

☙

Me and the Antichrist Conquer Walmart

I GOT A GOAT. Live in the country; get a goat, why not?

He's a rescue goat, pigmy, chocolate and white, nuts the size and color of ripe avocados. Bought him off a bunch of Mexicans up near China Grove where he was destined to become some kid's birthday barbeque. Cabrito they call it.

He was roped to a tractor tire with a dozen others.

Got him home. Asked him what he wanted to be known by, suggested Charlie but he'd have none of it.

"Mi nombre es Senior Seis Seis Seis," he says. "But my friends call me Sixty for short." (He's bilingual)

Antichristo. Can't argue with a man's name and knowing we're on the Countdown to Armageddon I didn't think it would hurt to align myself with the winning team, me in the role of Coon the Baptist to the soon-to-be-leader of all of Christendom.

Talked to him, turns out a couple of them—the Mexicans, not the goats—had been using the kitchen of a fish house restaurant in China Grove, where they worked days, to butcher Sixty's extended family after everybody else had gone home at night. They'd sneak in after the fish house had closed and slaughter the poor, miserable creatures and be out before the day staff came to work. But as a result of their unholy mixing of fish and flesh, a senior citizen ended up with goat gut dysentery after eating a contaminated Friday Night Senior Flounder Special, dropped dead in the hospital three days later and the place closed down.

The Mexicans decided it was time to get rid of the evidence so they put up a sign for the leftover widows and orphans. 196 Pesos later, I got a goat.

Smart goat. Real smart goat. Smarter than a Baptist.

I figured he was Catholic, with the Hispanic heritage and all, but turns out he's converted Buddhist, drinks his own urine, says it has something to do with maintaining his electrolyte balance, even more difficult for him to do because of the cheap goat chow I been feeding him. I told him times are tight, that I don't have the spare cash for genuine Purina. He understands, just thankful he's got a roof over his head and nobody stokin' up the spit.

Drinking your own piss, direct from the source as he does, requires a level of skill that most of us humans don't have, and it is a wonder to behold. Sixty will stick out his organ about three inches and then whiz in a clockwise spiral that always hits the corner of his mouth. I had a cousin once who whizzed off the front porch to similar effect. I asked Sixty if goats piss counterclockwise south of the equator and he said it was true, the Coriolis effect, no need to fight gravity, just go with the flow.

Me and Sixty, we spend our evenings plotting to make our grand entrance back into the real world.

Our conversations used to go long into the night but I never could get him to quit soiling the sheets so I had to move him to his own place. No doubt his bed wetting was related to childhood trauma.

I built him a little faux Swiss chateau like the one

Shirley Temple lived in, in the movie *Heidi*. It's got a portico so he can stick his head out to get some fresh air on a rainy day. (Goats don't like to get their heads wet. Neither do I, just one more thing we've found we have in common.) I put medieval arrow slots in the doors and windows like the ones they have at Notre Dame—never can tell when you might have to defend the homestead—and painted on a couple of gargoyles. Just seemed appropriate, him being the Antichrist and all.

I thought Sixty might be offended, not sharing my bed anymore but he says he's glad for it, says he was finding my constant whining and poor mouthing a bit tedious, and while he's at it, finds me more than a little misogynistic, which I thought a little odd coming from a goat. He said he enjoys his space, what he calls his 'me' time.

Lately, our conversations have been all business, sometimes at my place, sometimes at his, often over a glass of Two Buck Chuck when I can afford it. He was hell on my Riedel stemware so we're down to drinking out of jelly glasses but that's okay. My days of putting on airs is over and bad wine tastes the same no matter what you drink it from.

[Is that a platitude worth repeating? Bad wine tastes the same, no matter what you drink it from. Hmm?? Maybe. Could be a headline in there somewhere. I'll put it in my file, never know when Madison Avenue might come calling again.]

So Mel, the guy I met at the Church of Jesus Starbucks where I go to swipe the Sunday paper said, "Coon, he's just a goat."

"Au contraire my pseudo-intellectual atheist friend. Sixty is The Cure."

"Cure? Cure for what?"

"It."

"It, what?"

"It, *all*. That's what.

"It's policy that matters, not the details. We're going for total world domination, if not annihilation, at least the parts we don't like anyway."

I told him that I had posited it to Sixty and Sixty said let's go for it.

I asked Sixty if it was not a problem us wiping out half the Western world, him being a Buddhist and a vegan.

He said, nah, he doesn't despise anything as much as a Baptist and since he's with me and since it doesn't look like we're gonna get out of this hellhole we're in anytime soon, Sixty feels, as he said, "It's change we can believe in."

I heard Sixty say that and I was sold, ready to go. Leadership matters.

[Rough cut so far]

It's me and Sixty and a hundred thousand righteous goats who are fed up with fundamentalists of every ilk and the laissez faire capitalism the Tea Bags espouse. We'll start with the fundamentalist churches and the advertising agencies who vie for the title of Great Satan. Then we'll move on to Walmart and anybody else who gets in our way. It's a work in progress, but it's a plan and it's coming together fast.

We're still in the conceptual stages, no rules, no restraints, just let our minds wander. It all makes sense even when it doesn't make sense; that's the creative process in action.

So Sixty says, "If I'm going to cry havoc and unleash the Goats of War, run them wild amongst the masses of the Tea Klux Klan, I need hashish."

"Splain that to me," I said in my best Ricky Ricardo accent.

"Hashshashin is the etymological derivation of the word assassin. The Hashshashin were great warriors, Nizari Ismailis who captured and inhabited many mountain fortresses under the leadership of Hassan-i Sabbah. Hassan gave them hash and virgins. I'll get to the virgins part in a minute."

"How do you know that?" I was in wonder of the depth of this goat's understanding of both history and our popular culture.

"Marco Polo, man, you should read him some time."

So I Googled it and Sixty was right. (Told you he was smarter than a Baptist.)

Back to the hashish: "Buddy, all I got is that cheap ditch weed they grow down behind the prison camp, I ain't got a hash budget," I said to Sixty. "It's all I can do to keep you in genuine Purina since you quit eating the cheap stuff. And I wouldn't know where to get hash for a hundred thousand goats even if I tried. You and me, we're down to seeds and stems."

I passed the bong to Sixty.

He took a drag, hacked a couple of times and said that's some weak shit man. Asked, where's the Kush?

Said we could score some easy in Thailand but understood that might be outside the realm of possibility given our current economic position. He suggested Oakland for sure, since the city had already licensed a half dozen marijuana mega farms, and had heard that if you knew the right people you could get it on the street at the farmer's market every Thursday night in San Luis Obispo, explaining that the central valley of California had once been his home. Said he met Oprah, who has a weekend house in nearby Santa Barbara, before he escaped from her petting zoo. Headed south. Was going to hide out with the homeless in San Diego when he was snatched by a cabal of undocumented workers who were hightailing it to North Carolina.

"What about that redneck who lives over on Highway 49 in that 9,000 square foot house with the in-ground pool and the greenhouses in back?" he asked.

"Him? I'm told he grows fresh flowers for florists."

"Fresh flowers my ass. You don't think he got that McMansion, the Harley, the boat and the lake house, the vintage Mercedes, a stable of show horses and a steady stream of skank sashaying through his bedroom growing petunias, do you?"

I said I hadn't heard about all that, that I understood he grew flowers for Walmart.

"Walmart, my ass. Trust me. The man's got a dozen Mexicans growing weed. I know, because every time one of them had a birthday, they'd roast up a brother and pass around the moota they had smuggled off the compound to celebrate."

I took another hit, "Still, I can't afford that much hash,

no matter who's growing it."

Sixty puffed, "Okay, get his skiff, his trim. We can make do on his scrap. We'll bubble it out, make some resin rich kiv. Just keep them fucking Mexicans out of the picture. I don't trust 'em man."

I could sense it, Sixty was growing paranoid.

He tipped his head, indicating that he wanted another toke. He had started to hit the weed pretty hard and I was growing concerned. I had always suspected that his was the product of an abusive childhood and that it might be drug related—as every problem in America is. If I had the money, I'd look in to rehab. There's a good place in Pasadena, saw it on TV. Maybe he could share a room with Heidi Fleiss or Lindsay Lohan. But there's no time for that now, the situation in the world being desperate as it is. Got to keep up the vibrations, stay positive, don't stop the movement of Jah people, oh yeah.

I laid in another bud and flicked my Bic.

So I'm brainstorming with Sixty, "Where do we start, you the Antichrist, me your foot washing disciple? Where to, the Middle East? Jerusalem?"

He said Babylon, knows a woman there. Promised her he'd come back some day. Wants to give her a ride out of town.

I said I don't have gas money to Babylon, let's start with the Walmart in Concord. We can go scope it out.

So last Sunday morning I was in Walmart to pick up a few things, left Sixty on the back of the truck to run surveillance while I snatched a few maintenance items, an inner tube for the John Deere and energy saving fluorescent light bulbs which give off a garish green light that makes you sick to your stomach, but every penny counts here in The Basement of the Great Recession where me and Sixty reside.

I decide to go over to the grocery department to see if they had any Salmonella free eggs since my chickens are out of season and while there I notice an enchanting little Cabernet Sauvignon, 2/$4.99, which is a buck less than I've been paying at the Food Lion in Mt. Pleasant. I couldn't tell the vintage but decided to pick up a couple of bottles anyway, run it by Sixty, see what he thinks even though I know he prefers Opolo Vineyards' 2009 Paso Robles Mountain Zinfandel.

[You can pick up a bottle at http://www.opolo.com. While you're at it, me and Sixty would appreciate any contribution you can make – a half case, maybe?]

Got to the checkout, where this Walmart creature told me that I couldn't buy wine no matter how cheap it was until after 12 o'clock noon on Sunday. Got to wait until all the backwoods, bumfuck, dumb as cockroach fundamentalists were out of church. (I paraphrase the Walmart associate but that was the gist of it.)

Goddamn it! Goddamn it!

Let me explain it to you. I didn't want to be grocery shopping at Walmart in the first place. This ain't even a cheap Chateau Mouton we're talking about, more like Boone's Farm in a phony Bordeaux bottle. I'm trying to cope with this Great Recession thing, not let it get me down when this overweight-by-two-hundred pounds, greasy headed, World's Greatest Loser Wannabe reminds me that she is just following the rules and that, and I quote her here, "In the State of North Carolina, it is illegal to purchase alcoholic beverages between the hours of whatever a.m. and noon Sunday." She was reading off a little laminated card which she offered to me as evidence of her authority in the matter.

I fucking lost it. I stood there, eyeball to eyeball with the enemy. "It's Sharia law. And it doesn't make a damned if it comes from Osama bin Laden in a mosque in Poonstan or Bubba bin Laden at the Church of Jesus Starbucks. I'd about druther take my chances with Osama, since I know for sure he's got good sense, horribly misguided though he might have been. These religious nutcases running around here can't wipe their own ass without getting shit on their fingers and they think they ought to be telling me what to do? How to live my life? When to buy a bottle of wine? It's time to weed the garden. Get 'em all a one way ticket straight to heaven, right now, before they royally fuck it up for the rest of us, that's what I say."

There was a guy in line behind me wearing a Dale Earnhardt T-shirt with a buggy full of potted meat and Zesta Crackers and a hand full of ten-cent off coupons. He left. Quickly, without cashing in his ten cent off coupons.

The woman behind him started laughing her ass off. Probably a Jehovah.

The two hundred-pound-overweight-greasy-headed Walmart associate was incensed.

"Pardon me," she said with feigned aplomb, "I— eye—am a Christian. It is Walmart's rule, not mine."

"It is not Walmart's rule. It's a dumb-assed state law, out of some dumb-assed respect for nutcase fundamentalists passed by some chicken shit politician, and if every fucking one of them blew up and went to hell tomorrow, this place would be a lot better off.

The maybe-Jehovah was shaking her head in agreement. As long as there's no exchange of bodily fluids or sharing of cups and saucers among the races, Jehovah and his crew don't care what people drink or when they buy it and I suspect they've always harbored a deep and abiding hardon for Baptists of all ilks.

"You're right, it's a Christian thing," says the associate.

"No, it is *not* a Christian *thing*. There are still a few Christians who don't think they need to go around with their heads stuck up somebody else's ass, telling them how to live their lives. And if you're such a good Christian, why the fuck aren't you in church on this fine Sunday morning?"

"Because Walmart doesn't make allowances for religious affiliation. We all have to share the work equally regardless of race, creed or national origin. Plus, at the Race for the Lord Chapel over at Boogertown Shopping Center where I am a Speed Babe for Jesus, we share our communion with our Lord and Savior on Saturday nights, right after the . . . "

"Stop. Stop, stop, stop. Like I give a shit about Bubba Jesus. All I want to do is buy a bottle of wine and I've wasted too much precious gas money driving out here to go home empty handed."

But I did. Go home empty handed. Once again, the forces of evil had won. But not for long.

I've booked Sixty to Babylon. He's going to recruit a hoard of righteous followers, pick up his girlfriend, maybe make a kiv contact.

Pale goat. Pale rider.

The Revelation nears.

As I await his departure, and triumphant return, I sit here and ponder wistfully my great and abiding love for Sixty and the great and spiritual journey upon which we are about to embark. I reflect on the extraordinary promise of our One and Only Hope for Salvation, Mr. Six Six Six, Himself.

I reminisce about those late nights we used to share around our little 16 inch TV with our borrowed cable account.

Showtime. HBO. Sixty loved Dexter and Californication but his favorite was Weeds. His dream was to lay down Mary Louise Parker and give her the goat love he knew she always wanted.

Now that he is back in his own place, his nights outside, alone, with time to meditate and contemplate, he has given up electronic media and once again taken up cosmology, the origin and very nature of the universe, which he senses, innately. He travels with the stars, knows from moment to moment where they are and how they move, when they rise and when they fall. He can tell you the seasons and forecast the weather with uncanny accuracy. It comes naturally to him. He just knows.

He rises early to lick the morning dew off the grass. A strict vegan, he wastes nothing and shares his single, daily cup of chow with any rabbit who asks to partake of his bounty. A gentle bunny bump on the nose and Sixty makes space at the manger.

And for this reason, because he, himself, has experienced firsthand the evil of religious persecution as a Buddhist indentured to a tribe of blood-thirsty Catholics, a virgin mother raped by an unholy father he never knew, now risen from bondage to walk in harmony with those too weak to protect themselves, offering unconditional love to all the creatures who follow him—including the Guinea fowl who can be a little hard to get along with— because he knows in his heart what is right—my heart and spirit and soul will follow Sixty, the destroyer of Walmart, and Baptists, and Ad Agencies, all the days of my life.

He is the light that guideth me with his one great parable:

And Sixty Sayeth:

Expect others to do unto you
as you have done unto them.

Etch it in stone.
Sing it unto the heavens.
Oh happy day.
Oh holy day.
The End has ended and the Beginning has begun.
(Anybody seen my lighter?)

CR

Me and the Eternal Journey

I HAD BEEN TO A CONFERENCE IN MUNICH in early June and decided to drive to Saint-Tropez to spend a week on the beach before the season started. I had stopped for early dinner in St. Moritz, then down the laces to the bottom of the Alps at sunset, then on into the night planning to drive straight through and arrive in time to hobnob at late breakfast with the artistes and assorted snobs over a ham and cheese at Le Gorille.
[http://www.legorille.com]

It was late, the middle of the night. I had no idea where I was, mountains on the left and water on the right. I got out to stretch, take a leak, catch some air, and looked around and realized even in the dark that I was in the most beautiful place on the face of the earth.

I checked the map. It said I was on the shores of Lake Como.

I promised myself I'd come back some day.

Always wanted to. All my life.

Never made it.

Not yet anyway.

Perry was from there. Como.

The Medici summered there.

The Borgias and the renaissance popes had their hunting lodges near what is now the Hotel Bellagio.

Benito Mussolini was hung by his heels at a service

station on the north shore on his way to hook up with his buddy Adolf.

George Clooney hangs out there too. (I always thought that if they made a movie about Porfirio Rubirosa, George should be the man to play him. I like George.)

My expectations have changed since way back then, my life having taken a significant downturn. Like Dr. Hannibal Lecter in his cell in the basement of the insane asylum, I know they'll never let me out of here, not while I'm alive anyway, Clarice.

Never will I enjoy a studiolo of my very own on the lake, or perhaps a piccola stanza in someone's home, even if for just the summer.

Never will I sit alone with a glass of Sangiovese while the fishing boats tie up as the sun sets over the Piemonte.

A few gentle days by those bucolic waters is my last hope for this life, but unless the economy changes soon and hard, and my luck with it, none of which is likely to come to pass, never again will I stand on the romantic shores of Lago di Como.

I don't think I'll have a sequel.

All my flights have been cancelled.

Escape is not in the offing.

Like Dr. Lecter, I would gladly kill to get out of here but I don't know who. There just isn't anybody worth knocking off here on Prison Camp Road, not a single person whose life is worth a tourist class ticket out of town.

So this might be the next best thing.

I'm thinking, I could at least be *buried* there. Scattered

actually, and I'm trying to scrape together the funds.

It's never too early to plan for the end—as the mutual fund peddlers and variable annuity shysters I know all too well like to say.

Successful or not, I have always been a man with a plan. I have a cut-rate ceremony in mind, a simple bake and shake.

Let me bullet point it for you:

- Basic cremation here in the U.S.
- Cardboard box
- UPS to the Hotel Bellagio
- Slip the concierge 50 Euros and tell him to chuck my dust into the holy waters just outside his door

I figure a thousand dollars for the burn, fifty more for UPS.

[Hold on a minute! I might have just figured this whole thing out. Maybe UPS will want to do a commercial? Starring my box. Or instead of a plain, cardboard box, maybe they'll spring for a nice vase, an urn with their logo on it? Hey, it's a concept. The last ad I'll ever do. What do you think? Maybe I'll storyboard it and send it to them. You never know. Maybe. Maybe not. Back to the here and now.]

Fifty Euros more for incidentals. Twelve-hundred bucks ought to do it, depending on the exchange rate at the time. But that's twelve-hundred dollars I don't have.

On the other hand, 60 people at $20 a pop, that's all it takes. If you'd like to join me, figuratively speaking, whip out that Capitol One Card and punch in www.coonboy.com on your mobile computing device. You can PayPal it.

In the meantime, if by chance you run in to George and if by chance he's in need of a cook or gardener or a man's man, someone to schlep his bags, no doubt I am just what he's looking for. We could kill two birds with one stone so to speak. If you'd put in a good word for me, I'd sure appreciate it.

Grazie molto!

୯ଃ

Appendix: How true?

Although, legally perhaps, this book is a work of fiction, I am often asked if it is true. And the answer is, yes, it is. Maybe not Oprah Winfrey true, but certainly Jesus Christ true. How much true do you need? Did it really happen? Sure. For those of you who obsess over such things, here's the real truth, episode by episode.

Me
True.

Me and My Cousin's Red Speckled Balls
98%

Me and My Addiction
Completely. I changed a couple of names but no matter. I've still got the drawing. When asked what I would change about my life, what one thing started me on a regrettable career in advertising; it was the incident with the frog. But the car, just to ride in that car almost made it worth it.

Me and Spinning Dead Babies
I was a youngster and the grownup part is my recounting of what I remember hearing at the time, but it was as I remember it, and I remember it well.

Me and Poor Tilly
I've massaged a couple of the names. And I can't swear that Tilly never, ever, wore panties, but I know she didn't most of the time. I'm sure of it. I was tongue-tied too and never knew it, the result of constant ear infections as a child, which affected my hearing so that—by the time I learned to talk—I couldn't pronounce certain consonants, which meant I spoke in baby talk. Misses Swaringen was a good eight months pregnant at the time. I didn't mention that because I thought I might not be able to reconcile it with her clothes and her attraction to me. She was very fashionably dressed, perhaps the only woman I had ever seen in person who was so well attired. At the time, Johnny Carson's first TV show,

"Who Do You Trust?" was on right after school. [Now this is truly amazing. I just went to Wikipedia to confirm the name of the show and what does the first line say: "at 3:30 PM, Eastern - which helped garner a significant number of young viewers coming home from school." I kid you not.] So I would come home and immediately turn on Johnny Carson before he was famous and practice talking like him. Later, he lived in Malibu. I was there once at a garden shop where a friend's sister worked. She told me that he came there regularly and that she knew him fairly well. I asked her to thank him for me, for teaching me to speak clearly. I don't know if he ever got the message. I hope so.

Me and Barking Dogs
Yes.

Me and Junior, Jr.
Half of this is true and half is not, but in the whole, it is an accurate accounting both in fact and in spirit.

Me and the Ku Klux Klan and the Homecoming Queen
Every word. Since Sharon sat behind me in French class, which was her point of reference thirty years later, she thought it was cute to pretend to be sixteen again. I did not. It got old fast but thankfully our romance didn't last more than a couple of hours.

Me and the Terrorists at Starbucks, Part 1
I had Killer's email address planning to stay in touch but I somehow erased it inadvertently. And sadly, Mel passed away last summer, may he rest in peace. He is missed by all who knew him.

Me and the Terrorists at Starbucks, Part 2
See for yourself. Google Earth The Peachoid.

Me and the Terrorists at Starbucks, Part 3
Who knows? Let's hope not. But I fear it may come to pass. We've got to quit killing children to steal their oil. What would you say if you were there, in that city, in that plaza, on that day? I don't

think "I'm sorry" would quite cover the wrongs we've done to so many innocent people.

Me, in a Blue Moon
Yep. Mary Ann, are you there? Hope you're still happily married. If not, get in touch. I'd love to catch up. You were always the best. Miss you. Mean it.

Me and Mr. Vice President of Kiss My Ass
Sorry to say it is.

Me and Used Food
I've lost fifteen pounds to prove it.

Me and My Type
Well, yeah, I guess so.

Me and the Man of My Dreams
Yes, I do have all 50 of Popular Mechanics' Tools Every Man Should Own, and yes, I do know how to use them. I've never been to Venice in the winter. If you're in the mood and you've got an extra ticket, let me know. Front me a few bucks and I'll buy the Bellinis.

Me and the Antichrist Conquer Walmart
To be honest, Sixty's vocabulary is not as extensive as I've suggested, not his spoken vocabulary anyway. But I know him so well by now that I know what he is thinking. It's a special relationship and much of our communication is nonverbal. The facts? In fact, for me, this is the truest story of all.

Me and the Eternal Journey
We will see, won't we? I hope so. And if you know somebody who knows somebody who knows somebody who knows George, please, please, please, put in a good word for me.

Hope that helps to clear it all up,
CJB

Oh, and the one question I am asked over and over:
Does the Antichrist really exist?
Yes he does.
And he's back.
And he's not happy.

Conley J. Boyce is a Madison Avenue refugee, a former double espresso sipper who has taken his place among the poor, the pitiful and the downtrodden. He's a man with a grudge, living in, as he calls it, "The Basement of the Great Recession." And he does indeed reside in a white trash house trailer down the road from the prison camp with a heard of rabbits and Senior Seis Seis Seis, a goat known as the Antichrist.

You can reach him at Conley@CoonBoy.com

Coming Soon

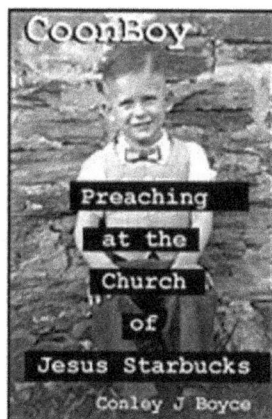

Preaching at the Church of Jesus Starbucks

Learn more, view sample chapters, free downloads

at

www.CoonBoy.com